LITURGICAL THEOLOGY OF ORTHODOX LITURGICAL MUSIC

In Memory of

Fr. Alexander Schmemann

(+ 1983),

and

Dedicated to

Dr. Paul Meyendorff.

Liturgical Theology of Orthodox Liturgical Music

By

David Barrett

Foreward by
Father Sergei Glagolev

Orthodox Liturgical Press
Southbury, Connecticut
January 2017

Library of Congress Cataloging-in-Publication Data

Barrett, David
1956 –

Conducting and Rehearsing Orthodox Liturgical Music

Library of Congress Control Number: 2016921617

LITURGICAL THEOLOGY OF ORTHODOX LITURGICAL MUSIC

Copyright © 2016 by
David Barrett

Orthodox Liturgical Press
Southbury, CT 06488

All Rights Reserved.

ISBN 978-0-9915905-4-4

Printed in the United States of America.

CONTENTS

FOREWORD — xv

PREFACE — xvii

1. THE ESSENCE OF LITURGICAL THEOLOGY — 1
   - A. THE ESSENCE OF LITURGY — 1
   - B. THE ESSENCE OF THEOLOGY — 6
   - C. THE ESSENCE OF LITURGICAL THEOLOGY — 10

2. MACRO LITURGICS AND MICRO LITURGICS — 15
   - A. MACRO LITURGICS — 15
   - B. MICRO LITURGICS — 17
   - C. THE RESURRECTION: THE QUINTESSENTIAL MACRO LITURGIC — 19
   - D. THE ESSENCE OF ORTHODOX LITURGICAL MUSIC — 26
   - E. ESSENTIAL LITURGICAL DUALISM: THE EUCHARIST AND THE LITURGY OF TIME — 30

3. VESPERS 33
- A. PSALM 103 — 33
- B. LITANIES — 36
- C. KATHISMATA — 38
- D. STIKHERA — 39
- E. "GLADSOME LIGHT" — 41
- F. EVENING PROKEIMENA — 44
- G. OLD / NEW TESTAMENT READINGS — 47
- H. MATINS GOSPEL — 48
- I. LITYA AND RESPONSES — 48
- J. CONCLUDING TROPARIA — 49
- K. PARISH VIGIL: A PROPOSED ORDO — 50

4. MATINS 55
- A. THE SIX PSALMS — 55
- B. LITANIES — 56
- C. "GOD IS THE LORD" OR "ALLELUIA!" AND TROPARIA — 57

D. KATHISMATA AND
    THE POLYELEOS   58

E. PSALM 137 AND
    THE MEGALYNARION   60

F. EVLOGITARIA, HYPAKOE,
    AND HYMNS OF DEGREES   61

G. PROKEIMENA   62

H. MATINS GOSPEL   63

I. "HAVING BEHELD THE
    RESURRECTION OF CHRIST,
    PSALM 50, AND
        TROPARION   64

J. THE KANON   65

K. THE EXAPOSTILARION   66

L. THE PRAISES   67

M. THE DOXOLOGY   68

N. THE LITURGICAL CENTRALITY
    OF MATINS   69

5. THE DIVINE LITURGY   71
    A. DOXOLOGY   71
    B. LITANIES   72
    C. THE ANTIPHONS   73
    D. THE THIRD ANTIPHON   74
    E. "COME, LET US WORSHIP"   75
    F. TROPARIA AND KONTAKIA   77
    G. THE TRISAGION   78
    H. THE PROKEIMENON   79
    I. THE EPISTLE   80
    J. "ALLELUIA" VERSES   82
    K. THE GOSPEL   83
    L. THE CHERUBIKON   84
    M. THE ANAPHORA   87
    N. THE LORD'S PRAYER   89
    O. THE KOINONIKON   90
    P. "HAVING BEHELD
        THE RESURRECTION
            OF CHRIST"   93
    Q. LITURGY ENDING   94

6. SACRAMENTAL SERVICES 95
    A. HOLY BAPTISM 96
    B. HOLY MATRIMONY 103
    C. FUNERAL 107

7. THE FESTAL CYCLE 117
    A. VESPERAL LITURGY 117
    B. VIGILS OF THE NATIVITY OF CHRIST AND OF THEOPHANY 120

8. LENT, HOLY WEEK, AND PASCHA 129
    A. FORGIVENESS VESPERS 129
    B. KANON OF ST. ANDREW OF CRETE 131
    C. THE LITURGY OF THE PRESANCTIFIED GIFTS 134
    D. BRIDEGROOM MATINS 147
    E. MATINS OF HOLY THURSDAY 156

F. VESPERAL LITURGY OF HOLY THURSDAY	159
G. MATINS OF HOLY FRIDAY	166
H. ROYAL HOURS OF HOLY FRIDAY	176
I. VESPERS OF HOLY FRIDAY	177
J. MATINS OF HOLY SATURDAY	153
K. VESPERAL LITURGY OF HOLY SATURDAY	192
L. NOCTURNS OF HOLY SATURDAY	203
M. PASCHAL MATINS	206
N. PASCHAL DIVINE LITURGY	216
O. PASCHAL VESPERS	225
P. PASCHAL HOURS	229
Q. BRIGHT WEEK	229

9. DEVELOPMENT OF
    LITURGICAL THEOLOGY   231
    A. LITURGICAL RESEARCH   231
    B. LITURGICAL PUBLICATIONS   232
    C. LITURGICAL SYMPOSIUMS   233

BIBLIOGRAPHY   235

FOREWARD

The study of liturgical theology enables us to enter into the life of the Church, to understand our relationship with God and all the saints. Liturgical theology is the language of the Church.

This book speaks to the subject of liturgical theology in a way that we can relate to. It brings liturgical theology alive in our discourse. It keeps within the practice, experience, and Holy Tradition of the Church. David Barrett presents the application of liturgical theology to Orthodox liturgical music brilliantly.

Fr Sergei Glagolev
East Meadow, NY
January 2017

Fr Sergei Glagolev is a renowned music teacher and composer of Orthodox liturgical music.

PREFACE

This present opus is a book that examines the liturgical theology of Orthodox liturgical music, and, furthermore, looks at the theological dimension of how the musical aspect of our services functions liturgically. To say that this type of a work has been needed for a long time would be an understatement. However, serious, informed, theological discussions of these topics **have** been occurring for many years among Church musicians, liturgical theologians, liturgists, clergy, choir directors, etc. It is the hope that this book will spur on further discussions and (hopefully) constructive action regarding our liturgical life. This is why it was written.

First of all, it is necessary to give a brief, albeit clear, presentation on the essence of liturgical theology. This is necessary because, as the name suggests, liturgical music is, first, foremost, and essentially, *liturgical*. Then, in parallel to this, there will be an examination into the concepts of macro liturgics and micro liturgics. Third, we will look at the ontology (the very being) of liturgical music in its varied dimensions (liturgical, musical, evolutionary, missionary, and eschatological). After this, the remaining three chapters will present an examination of the key basic services of the Orthodox Church that may be celebrated the year round in parishes: Vespers, Matins, and the Divine Liturgy.

May the Lord God provide all of us with the seriousness, open-mindedness, and prayerfulness that are vital to our liturgical ministries, to His glory and the glory of His holy Kingdom!

1
THE ESSENCE OF LITURGICAL THEOLOGY

In order to understand liturgical theology and its relationship to Orthodox liturgical music, we must first understand the essence each of liturgy, theology, and liturgical theology.

A. THE ESSENCE OF LITURGY

A very fitting and apt description on the essence of liturgy has been given by Father Thomas Hopko:

"The Church may be defined as the new life in Christ. It is man's life lived by the Holy Spirit in unison with God. All aspects of the new life of the Church participate in the mystery of salvation. In Christ and the Holy Spirit(,) everything which is sinful and dead becomes holy and alive by the power of God the Father. And(,) so(,) in Christ and the Holy Spirit(,) everything in the Church becomes a sacrament, an element of the mystery of the Kingdom of God as it is already being experienced in the life of this world."[1]

This is made even more abundantly clear by Father Alexander Schmemann:

"If assembling as the Church is, in the most profound sense of the term, the **beginning** of the eucharistic celebration, its first and fundamental condition, then its **end** and completion is the Church's entrance into (H)eaven, her fulfillment at the table of Christ, in (H)is (K)ingdom. It is imperative to indicate and to confess this as the sacrament's end, purpose and fulfillment immediately after confessing the 'assembly as the Church' as its beginning because this 'end' also reveals the unity of the (E)ucharist, its order and essence as movement and ascent – as, above all and before all, the sacrament of the (K)ingdom of God. And it is no accident, of course, that in its present

---

[1] Hopko, Thomas, *The Orthodox Faith: Volume II: Worship*, 2nd Edition, Department of Religious Education, Orthodox Church in America, SVS (St Vladimir's Seminary) Press, Yonkers, NY (hereafter referred to as "*Worship*"), p. 30.

form the (L)iturgy begins with the solemn blessing of the (K)ingdom."[2]

Liturgy is *not*, as some may think, a religious escape from the world. Nor it is a religious "play" somehow "depicting" the life of Christ. Even less is it a set of mystical and foggy "symbols" that is supposed to "represent" something "other-worldly." Rather, it *is* our entrance into the Kingdom of God, that Kingdom that is yet to come, **already** in **this** world at **this** time and place. And the **content** of that Kingdom is our life in Christ, which is expressed and experienced **liturgically**:

"Christianity is neither a philosophy nor a morality nor a ritual, but the **gift of a new life** in Christ, and this new life is the Church. In it, we who 'now have received mercy' (I Pet. 2:10) constitute a new nation under God, which offers to God spiritual thanks and offering, carries on His work in the world,

---

[2] Schmemann, Alexander, *The Eucharist: Sacrament of the Kingdom*, SVS Press, Crestwood, NY, 1988 (hereafter referred to as "*Eucharist*"), p. 27 (emphasis in the original).

is a witness of salvation and grows in the knowledge of Truth and Grace; hence the unique place and function of liturgy in its life. Liturgical services are not one of the 'aspects' of the Church; they express its very essence, are its breath, its heartbeat, its constant self-revelation. Through the sacraments and especially through the sacrament of the Holy Eucharist, the Church, as one theologian worded it, always 'becomes that which it is,' i.e., the Body of Christ, a new unity of men in Him. Liturgy implies above all the **gathering of the faithful**, yet the word **Church** itself means precisely **gathering**, 'where two or three are gathered….' In this gathering and through it we, 'though many, are one body' (I Cor. 12:12). Through liturgy we enter into communion with the Word of God, learn to know His will, remember the death and (R)esurrection of Christ, and receive the gifts of the Holy Spirit, indispensible for our Christian life and action in this world."[3]

---

[3] Schmemann, Alexander, *Liturgy and Life: Christian Development through Liturgical Experience*, Department of Religious Education, Orthodox Church in America, New York, NY, 1983 (hereafter referred to as "*Liturgy and Life*"), pp. 12-13 (emphasis in the original).

Thus, liturgy constitutes the ontology of the Church, makes her what she is, fulfills her being and purpose. It is the ***ascent***, ***our*** ascent, from the confines of "this world" to the ***experience*** and ***reality*** of the Kingdom of God:

"The (D)ivine (L)iturgy – the continual ascent, the lifting up of the Church to ***(H)eaven***, to the throne of glory, to the unfading light and joy of the (K)ingdom of God – is the focus of this experience, simultaneously its source and presence, gift and fulfillment. 'Standing in the temple of (T)hy glory(,) we think we are in (H)eaven.' These words are not pious rhetoric, for they express the very essence, the very purpose of both the Church and of her worship as above all precisely a ***liturgy***, an action (εργον), in which the essence of what is taking place is simultaneously revealed and fulfilled. But in what is this essence, in what is the ultimate meaning of the (D)ivine (L)iturgy if not in the manifestation and the granting to us of this divine good? From where, if not from our 'Lord, it is good for us to be here,' comes its simultaneously otherworldly, heavenly, and cosmic beauty, that ***wholeness***, in which ***all*** – words, sounds, colors, time, space, movement, and the ***growth*** of all of them – is revealed, realized as the renewal of creation, as ours, as the ascent of the entire world on high, to where Christ has raised and is eternally raising us?"[4]

This, then, is the essence of liturgy, as taught, proclaimed, and *experienced* in the Orthodox Church.

B. THE ESSENCE OF THEOLOGY

The essence of theology, as attested to by Vladimir Lossky and other Orthodox theologians, lies in the mystical experience of our membership in the Church, revealed primarily through liturgical worship:

"The (E)astern tradition has never made a sharp distinction between mysticism and theology; between personal experience of the divine mysteries and the dogma affirmed by the Church….To put it another way, we must live the dogma expressing a

---

[4] *Eucharist*, pp. 165-166 (emphasis in the original).

revealed truth, which appears to us as an unfathomable mystery, in such a fashion that instead of assimilating the mystery to our mode of understanding, we should, on the contrary, look for a profound change, an inner transformation of spirit, enabling us to experience it mystically. Far from being mutually opposed, theology and mysticism support and complete each other. One is impossible without the other. If the mystical experience is a personal working out of the content of the common (F)aith, theology is an expression, for the profit of all, of that which can be experienced by everyone."[5]

The same idea was expressed by Father John Meyendorff, in his own unique style:

"Because the concept of ***theologia*** in Byzantium, as with the Cappodocian (f)athers, was inseparable from ***theoria*** ('contemplation'), theology could not be – as it was in the West - a rational deduction from 'revealed' premises, i.e., from Scripture or from the statements of an ecclesiastical

---

[5] Lossky, Vladimir, *The Mystical Theology of the Eastern Church*, SVS Press, Crestwood, NY, 2002 (hereafter referred to as "*Mystical Theology*"), pp. 8-9.

magisterium; rather, it was a vision experienced by the saints, whose authority was, of course, to be checked against the witness of Scripture and Tradition....The true theologian was the one who saw and experienced the content of his theology; and this experience was considered to belong not to the intellect alone (although the intellect was not excluded from its perception), but to 'the eyes of the Spirit,' which place the whole man – intellect, emotions, and even senses – in contact with divine existence....Revelation, therefore, was limited neither to the written documents of Scripture, nor to conciliar definitions, but was directly accessible, as a living truth, to a human experience of God's presence in His Church."[6]

Father Thomas Hopko verifies this in his section on "The Liturgy" in his book, **Doctrine**:

"The living experience of the Christian sacramental and liturgical life is a primary source of

---

[6] Meyendorff, John, *Byzantine Theology: Historical Trends and Doctrinal Themes*, Fordham University Press, New York, NY, 1983 (hereafter referred to as *"Byzantine Theology"*), pp. 8-9 (emphasis in the original).

Christian doctrine. In the liturgy of the Church, the Bible and the Holy Tradition come alive and are given to the living experience of the Christian people. Thus, through prayer and sacramental worship(,) men are 'taught by God' as it was predicted for the messianic age (John 6:45). In addition to the living experience of the liturgy, the texts of the services and sacraments provide a written source of doctrine in that they may be studied and contemplated by one who desires an understanding of Christian teachings."[7]

Therefore, along with other "sources" of Holy Tradition (Scripture, the patristic writings, iconography, canon law), the liturgical services and their content (prayers, exclamations, hymnography) provide another "source" of doctrine and theology in the Church.

---

[7] Hopko, Thomas, *The Orthodox Faith: Volume I: Doctrine*, 2nd Edition, Department of Religious Education, Orthodox Church in America, SVS Press, Yonkers, NY (hereafter referred to as "*Doctrine*"), p. 27.

C. THE ESSENCE OF LITURGICAL THEOLOGY

As Father Alexander Schmemann, who has been appropriately referred to as "the father of liturgical theology," pointed out in his writings again and again, liturgy theology is not the "theology of liturgy," of its various aspects and forms, of what liturgy "is" and is supposed "to be." Rather, liturgical theology deals with the Faith itself as revealed in liturgy, **what liturgy says <u>about</u> the Faith!** He would come to clarify this time and time again:

"In the approach which I advocate by every line I ever wrote, the question addressed by liturgical theology to liturgy and to the entire liturgical tradition is not about liturgy but about 'theology,' i.e. about the (F)aith of the Church as expressed, communicated and preserved by the liturgy. Here(,) liturgy is viewed as the ***locus theologicus par excellence*** because in its very function, its ***leitourgia*** in the original meaning of that word, to manifest and to fulfill the Church's (F)aith and to manifest it not partially, not 'discursively,' but as living totality and catholic experience. And it is because liturgy is that living totality and that catholic experience by the Church of her own (F)aith that it is the very **source** of theology, the condition that makes it **possible**. For(,) if theology, as the Orthodox Church maintains, is not a mere sequence of more or less individual interpretations of this or that 'doctrine' in the light and thought forms of this or that 'culture' and 'situation,' but the attempt to express Truth itself, to find words adequate to the mind and experience of the Church, then it must of necessity have its source where the (F)aith, the mind, and the experience of the Church have their living focus and expression, where faith in both essential meanings of that word, as Truth revealed and given, as Truth accepted and 'lived,' has its **epiphany**, and that is precisely the function of the **leitourgia**.[8]

The main ontological aspect of the Church as being **eschatological**, of concerning itself above all else with the "Last Things," with the Kingdom of God, is precisely what is manifested in liturgy:

---

[8] Schmemann, Alexander, *Liturgy and Tradition: Theological Reflections of Alexander Schmemann*, Thomas Fisch, Editor, SVS Press, Crestwood, NY, 1990, (hereafter referred to as "*Liturgy and Tradition*"), p. 40 (emphasis in the original).

"What is important for us at this point is the relationship between this cosmic and eschatological nature of the Church and her *leitourgia*. For(,) it is precisely in and through her liturgy – this being the latter's specific and unique 'function' – that the Church is **informed** of her cosmic and eschatological vocation, **receives** the power to fulfill it and thus truly **becomes** 'what she is' – the sacrament, in Christ, of the new creation; the sacrament, in Christ, of the Kingdom. In this sense the liturgy is indeed 'means of grace,' not in the narrow and individualistic meaning given this term in post-patristic theology, but in the all-embracing meaning, as means of always making the Church what she is – a realm of grace, a communion with God, of new knowledge and new life. The liturgy of the Church is cosmic and eschatological because the Church is cosmic and eschatological; but the Church would not have been cosmic and eschatological had she not been given, as the very source and constitution of her life and (F)aith, the **experience** of the new creation, the experience and **vision** of the Kingdom which is to come. And this is precisely the *leitourgia* of the Church's cult, the function which makes it the source and indeed the very **possibility** of theology.[9]

---

[9] Ibid, pp. 57-58 (emphasis in the original).

Father Schmemann also clearly defines the methodology of liturgical theology:

"If the **object** of liturgical theology which I have attempted to describe and define in an obviously very general and even superficial manner is thus acknowledged, the method poses no real problems. It consists of three steps:

"1) In the first step the question is to establish **the liturgical fact**....

"2) The second step is that of **theological analysis** of this liturgical fact. Whether it concerns a feast or a sacramental rite, a text or a celebration, the theological 'content' or 'coefficient' of each of these liturgical components requires that each be situated in the theological context which is proper to it in order to be understood and defined....

"3) The third and, obviously, most important step is that of synthesis, the release of the inherent theological meaning from the witness of the liturgical **epiphany** itself."[10]

---

[10] *Liturgy and Tradition*, p. 144 (emphasis in the original).

This, then, is the essence of liturgical theology and, therefore, the task of the Orthodox liturgical musician.

2
MACRO LITURGICS AND MICRO LITURGICS

There are two vitally important ways to look at, study, and evaluate the specifics of our liturgical services: macro liturgics and micro liturgics.

A. MACRO LITURGICS

Macro liturgics is the method of studying elements or groups of elements from the liturgical *ordo* of services. As the name implies, this encompasses large portions of the services.

For example, one group of liturgical elements that goes together to make a unified "set" is the group that involves the Scriptural elements at the Divine Liturgy. This begins with the Prokeimenon, which introduces the Epistle reading, then the Epistle reading itself, followed by the "Alleluia!"

Verses, which introduce the Gospel reading,[11] the Gospel reading itself, and, finally, the Sermon. These five elements comprise one liturgical "unit," so to speak. In the ancient Church, both the Prokeimenon and the "Alleluia!" Verses, like other elements of the Divine Liturgy, were celebrated in what is called the **"*responsorial Psalmody*"** format, that is, the people would sing a refrain from the Psalm and then a reader would chant the verses of the Psalm *in their entirety*, one at a time, between the singing of the refrain.[12] So, for example, the Resurrectional Prokeimenon in tone 1 comes from Psalm 32,[13] which has twenty-two verses. The people would begin by singing the refrain, then they would sing it twenty-two more times, once after each chanting of a Psalm verse by the reader.

The same is true for the "Alleluia!" Verses. Staying with a Sunday where tone 1 is celebrated,

---

[11] Hopko, Thomas, Podcast series *Worship in Spirit and Truth*, Ancient Faith Radio, podcast for 18 September 2013, "Allelujah, Allelujah, Allelujah."

[12] Taft, SJ, Robert F., *Beyond East and West: Problems in Liturgical Understanding*, Second Revised and Enlarged Edition, Pontifical Oriental Institute, Rome, Italy, 2011 (hereafter referred to as "*Beyond East and West*"), p. 197.

[13] The Psalms are here numbered according to the Septuagint.

the reader would, in the ancient Church, chant a *triple* "Alleluia!", and the people would respond by singing a *triple* "Alleluia!". The reader would then chant the verses of the Psalm *in their entirety*, one at a time, between the singing of the *triple* "Alleluia!". Here, for the Sunday of tone 1, the reader would chant, one-by-one, all fifty verses of Psalm 17. This longer rendering of the Prokeimenon and the "Alleluia!" Verses in the "responsorial Psalmody" format was done in order to prepare the people spiritually for hearing the Scriptural readings in the Epistle and the Gospel, respectively. It is done that way today in many monasteries, and some parishes are beginning to implement this early Church restoration.

B. MICRO LITURGICS

Micro liturgics is the study of elements or groups of elements in the liturgical services occurring simultaneously. As the name suggests, this involves liturgical elements occupying a small amount of time in the services.

One example of this is the Entrance Hymn for the Vesperal Liturgy of Holy Saturday. Some arrangements of this hymn are in a melismatic setting, that is, having multiple notes per word or syllable. Other settings that have misaccentuation of the text could have this problem resolved by adding more notes (longer melismas) to the setting. Some people question doing this because of the procession that will occur during the Entrance. However, what these people forget is that the Eucharistic Entrance for this particular Vesperal Liturgy, just like the entrance for the Presanctified Liturgy, has **no** commemorations made. The entire Entrance is done by the clergy and the servers in ***total silence***. Therefore, if a few extra notes for an extended melisma *is* called for, there is not the usual concern that there will be not enough time for the clergy to do the commemorations before the Entrance procession concludes because, once again, there are **no** commemorations chanted.[14] This is a good illustration of how the elements of micro liturgics interact with one another and can lead to intelligent decisions regarding the celebration of the services.

---

[14] Please see my forthcoming *Composing and Arranging Orthodox Liturgical Music*, OLP (Orthodox Liturgical Press), publication date July 2017, for a further-detailed explanation of this example.

Some people misuse these two terms. They use the term "macro liturgics" to refer to elements that are appropriate for liturgical services and "micro liturgics" to refer to elements that are not appropriate for liturgical services. It seems more appropo to refer to the former elements (those that *are* appropriate for liturgical services) as "liturgical" and the latter elements (those that are *not* appropriate for liturgical services) as "para-liturgical," and leave the terms "macro liturgics" and "micro liturgics" to be used as presented here.

C. THE RESURRECTION: THE QUINTESSENTIAL MACRO LITURGIC

The concept of macro liturgics goes beyond just large portions of the liturgical services. In fact, in its ultimate size, it encompasses the entire liturgical year itself.

Pascha, the Resurrection of our Lord, God, and Savior, Jesus Christ, is the quintessential macro liturgic! It is the Feast of feasts, around which everything in the liturgical year and all the services revolve. While the Sundays of the liturgical year are numbered as a certain Sunday after Pentecost (due to bringing the fulness of the Kingdom, which Pentecost celebrates, to the "regular time" of this fallen world), the Resurrection remains **the** focal center of the liturgical year (the Oktoechos cycle of the eight tones begins anew each year on Pascha, starting with tone 1):

"Although the first of September is considered the start of the Church year, according to the Orthodox Church calendar, the real liturgical center of the annual cycle of Orthodox worship is the feast of the Resurrection of Christ. All elements of Orthodox liturgical piety point to and flow from Easter, the celebration of the new Christian Passover. Even the 'fixed feasts' of the Church(,) such as Christmas and Epiphany(,) which are celebrated according to a fixed date on the calendar(,) take their liturgical form and inspiration from the Paschal feast."[15]

"This is the starting point of our understanding of the sanctification of time. It is the Orthodox experience, which goes back to the (A)postles

---

[15] *Worship*, p. 72.

Development of Liturgical Theology

themselves, that in the center of our liturgical life, in the very center of that time which we measure as *year*, we find the **Feast of Christ's Resurrection**. What is Resurrection? Resurrection is the appearance in this world, completely dominated by time and(,) therefore(,) by death, of life that shall have no end. The One (W)ho (R)ose again from the dead does not die anymore. In this world of ours, not somewhere else, not in any 'other' world, there appeared one morning (S)omeone (W)ho is beyond death and yet *in* our time. This meaning of Christ's Resurrection, this great joy, is the central theme of Christianity; and it has been preserved in its fullness in the liturgy of the Orthodox Church. There is much truth expressed by those who say that the central theme of Orthodoxy, the center of all its experience, the frame of reference for everything else in her, is the **Resurrection of Christ**....Though it may seem strange to you, it is important to realize that every Sunday is a little Easter. I say 'Little Easter,' but it is really 'Great Easter.' Every week the Church comes to the same central experience: 'Having beheld the Resurrection of Christ...' Every Saturday night, when the priest carries the Gospel from the altar to the center of the church, after he has read the Gospel of the Resurrection, the same fundamental fact of our Christian (F)aith is proclaimed: CHRIST IS

RISEN!...This is the heart of our (F)aith; and it is only the reference to Pascha, as the end of all merely natural time and the beginning of the **new** time, that we can understand the whole liturgical year."[16]

"The Church is the entrance into the (R)isen life of Christ; it is communion in life eternal, 'joy and peace in the Holy Spirit.' And it is the expectation of the 'day without evening' of the Kingdom; not of any 'other world,' but of the fulfillment of all things and all life in Christ....But(,) I know that in Christ this great Passage, the **Pascha** of the world has begun, that the light of the 'world to come' comes to us in the joy and peace of the Holy Spirit, for **Christ is (R)isen and life reigneth**."[17]

"It is the worship of the Church that was(,) from the very beginning and still is(,) our entrance our entrance into, our communion with, the **new life of the Kingdom**. It is through her liturgical life that the Church reveals to us something that which 'the ear has not heard, the eye has not seen, and what

---

[16] *Liturgy and Life*, pp. 76-77 (emphasis in the original).
[17] Schmemann, Alexander, *For the Life of the World: Sacraments and Orthodoxy*, SVS Press, Crestwood, NY, 2002 (hereafter referred to as "*For the Life of the World*"), p. 106 (emphasis in the original).

Development of Liturgical Theology

has not yet entered the heart of man, but which God has prepared for those who love Him.' And(,) in the center of that liturgical life, as its heart and climax, as the sun whose rays penetrate everywhere, stands **Pascha**. It is the door opened every year into the splendor of God's Kingdom, the foretaste of the eternal joy that awaits us, the glory of the victory which already, although invisibly, fills the whole creation: 'death is no more!' The entire worship of the Church is organized around Easter, and(,) therefore(,) the liturgical year, i.e., the sequence of seasons and feasts, becomes a journey, a pilgrimage towards Pascha, the **End**, which is at the same time the **Beginning:** the end of all that which is 'old'; the beginning of the new life, a constant 'passage' from 'this world' into the Kingdom already revealed in Christ."[18]

So, we can see, from these excellent examples, that Pascha, the Resurrection of Christ, is at the heart of our liturgical year. Yet, it is even deeper than this. Christ's Resurrection, His **Pascha**, permeates the very services themselves, even those

---

[18] Schmemann, Alexander, *Great Lent: Journey to Pascha*, SVS Press, Crestwood, NY, 1974 (hereafter referred to as *"Great Lent"*), p. 13 (emphasis in the original).

that we deem, in our hearts and our minds, to be "negative," "sad," or dealing with things of the "fallen" world. The following two examples illustrate this point clearly.

First of all, both the Funeral service and the Memorial, after the initial doxology ("Blessed is our God…!") and the singing of the Trisagion, go immediately into the singing of "Alleluia!", with interspersed verses chanted by the priest. And the singing of "Alleluia!" is **always** a liturgical expression of **joy!**[19] Furthermore, towards the end of both the Funeral and the Memorial, there is a prayer the priest chants that begins, "O God of spirits and of all flesh…!" And the exclamation of this prayer begins, "For, **You** (meaning, Christ) **are the <u>Resurrection</u>**, the Life, and the Repose of Your servant, _____, O Christ our God…!".

The second example is from the Vespers of Holy Friday. Everyone will agree that this is **the** most solemn day of the entire liturgical year, the day of Christ's Crucifixion on the Cross! Nothing can be considered more "negative," "sad," or "fallen" than this world's rejection of our Lord and His murder by the most shameful death imaginable on the Cross.

---

[19] Ibid, p. 138, note 5.

Yet, in the midst of all this "negativity," "sadness," and "fallenness," the light of **the Resurrection** still shines *liturgically*! This is celebrated at the singing of the stikhera on the Apostikha, where the verses interspersed by the reader are **the same exact <u>resurrectional</u> verses chanted by the reader at every Saturday evening <u>Resurrectional</u> Vespers throughout the liturgical year:** "The Lord is King! He is robed in majesty!"; "For, He has established the world, so that it will never be moved!"; and, "Holiness befits Your house, O Lord. Forevermore!". Therefore, even here, in the midst of the pathos of Christ's Crucifixion, His Resurrection begins to shine forth for us!

Now, what does all this mean for choir directors and Church singers? Well, if the light of Christ's Resurrection shines through every liturgical nook and cranny of all the services of the liturgical year, then, to properly follow the liturgical theology of the Orthodox Church, **<u>all</u> the singing at <u>all</u> of the services of the entire liturgical year should be sung <u>resurrectionally</u>!** This does **not** mean that we should sing "Open the Doors of Repentance" and the Kanon of St Andrew of Crete in a boistrous manner. But, it <u>**does**</u> mean that we should sing these and all other hymnology not in a defeatist, morbid manner, but keeping the joy, the hope, and the faith of Christ's

Resurrection in mind! One way to do this is to pitch the music in a higher key, to get a "brighter" sound. Another way is, without rushing the pace of the singing, to move it along so that the "rhythm" of the service doesn't drag, in order for the service itself to be imbued with some life and energy. This is the first and most essential element of our liturgical theology as it applies to the celebration of our services in the singing of our Orthodox liturgical music!

D. THE ESSENCE OF ORTHODOX LITURGICAL MUSIC

Based on all that has been presented here, there are some affirmations and conclusions that can be stated regarding the essence of Orthodox liturgical music.

First and foremost, the name "liturgical music" manifests the ontological reality of this music: that it is primarily, and exclusively, **liturgical!** Its *raison d'etre* is precisely to be an artistically expressive component of the worship in the liturgical services of the Church. Granted, a choir or choral group **may** sing hymnological selections at concerts outside the services themselves; these "concerts" may even take place in the parish church building itself. Yet, at *that* point, the music ceases to be *liturgical* and becomes just another concert "piece" that may be sung alongside Handel's "Messiah." It is *only* in the context of the liturgical services that this hymnology fulfills its true function.

Second, since the liturgical services are in total harmony with the Scriptures, the dogmas, and the Holy Tradition of the Church, Orthodox liturgical music not only becomes a mode of expression of the theology of the Church, but its very manner of celebration must be in total harmony with that theology. We have already spoken above about how Pascha, the Feast of feasts celebrating the Resurrection of Christ, is the theological nexus of the liturgical year, and that, therefore, the singing of our liturgical music should be done in a paschal manner. Other aspects of the very being of the Church should also be manifested in the celebration of our liturgical music. For example, keeping in mind our Lord's command to "make disciples of all nations, baptizing them in the Name of the Father, and of the Son, and of the Holy Spirit" (Mt 28:19), another ontological aspect of the Church is her *missionary* calling. *Therefore*, the manner in which the liturgical music is celebrated will be specific to the time and place in which the Church (especially as found in the local parish) finds herself. The "style" and manner of Church singing in a 21st-century parish in America should certainly be different from an 18-century parish in Russia or a 16th-century parish in Antioch! This also influences how our hymnology is composed and arranged. The specific melodic arrangements, whether they be from a "traditional" chant system (such as Byzantine or Kievan) or a free-composed melody, as well as the essential nuances of text settings, are all vital elements in the missionary component of Church singing. For instance, artificially "stuffing" an English text into a musical setting that was arranged for Greek or Slavonic, will make the setting unintelligible and unprayerful. Taking the time and effort to set English texts to the music in such a way as to correctly accentuate the text and enhance its inherent meaning will reap rich liturgical rewards in the clarity, intelligibility, prayerfulness, and liturgical function of the hymnology.

As mentioned in the previous chapter, an essential component of our liturgical worship is its **eschatological dimension**. Again, all aspects of our liturgical music, from its composition, arrangement, and style of celebration, should manifest this eschatological ontology of liturgy and lift the members of the worshipping community to the reality of the Kingdom of God.

Third, Orthodox liturgical music should be formatted and celebrated according to its ***liturgical function!*** For instance, all litanies have a dialogical aspect to them, where the priest or deacon chants the petition, and the worshipping community responds with its word of affirmation, be it "Lord, have mercy," "To You, O Lord," or "Amen." Distinct from this, the times of liturgical worship that center around movement and action, such as processions, entrances, and the receiving of Holy Communion, have traditionally been accompanied by responsorial Psalmody, especially in the early Church. The specific function of the liturgical component being celebrated at any given moment of the services therefore determines the type, format, and function of the liturgical hymnology accompanying that component. This crucial and symbiotic relationship between function of liturgical component and format of liturgical music was, alas, lost in the consciousness of the Church for a long time, and has recently (thank God!) been rediscovered by Church liturgists and musicians.

E. ESSENTIAL LITURGICAL DUALISM: THE EUCHARIST AND THE LITURGY OF TIME

There is an essential liturgical dualism that exists in the Church. What is key to remember is that **this liturgical dualism has lived in the Church from the very beginning!**[20] This dualism consists of the presence of the Eucharist, which is the manifestation of the Kingdom of God here on Earth and, therefore, of the Eschaton, that which will be consummated at the Parousia for all eternity, and, at the same time, the presence of the Liturgy of Time, of those services that sanctify the time of our life in this world, here and now. As Fr Schmemann points out in the pages of his book referenced in the footnote below, many liturgiologists mistakenly thought that the Liturgy of Time was incompatible with the *eschatology* of the Church, that eschatology was a renunciation of the world that had chosen autonomy from God, sin, and death over communion with God, and that, therefore, the

---

[20] Schmemann, Alexander, *Introduction to Liturgical Theology*, SVS Press, Crestwood, NY, 1986, pp. 4-89, especially pp. 64-80.

Liturgy of Time could only have developed in the flowering of monasticism in the 4th century. Fr Schmemann corrects this skewed perspective by showing that, just as the New Testament is the fulfillment of the Old Testament, the Christian concept of eschatology fulfills the Jewish concept of eschatology. Both the Jews and the Christians awaited the coming of the Messiah. The "newness" of Christianity was that this awaiting was now fulfilled in the coming of Christ. Yet, the Kingdom **still** awaits **complete** fulfillment in the Second Coming of Christ. Therefore, since the current time of the Church is dualistic in the sense that the Kingdom is "already" here but "not yet" fulfilled, so this dualism is expressed **liturgically** with **both** the Sacrament of the Kingdom, the Eucharist, **and** the Liturgy of Time simultaneously taking place in the life of the Church. This dualism, since it is liturgical, therefore goes to the heart of the essence of the liturgical services: those of the Liturgy of Time (Vespers, Matins, etc.) function for us as we Christians being *in statio*, that is, in that state of watchfulness that Christ commanded us to be in, since we would not know when the Master would be coming **again the _second_ time!** In fact, our daily lives contain an experience, on a daily basis, of the Death and Resurrection of Christ: we experience a death each night when we enter that state of unconsciousness called "sleep," and we experience a resurrection each morning when we wake up, fully alive for a new day. Perhaps that is why, with the Resurrection of Christ being **the** central event in the life of the Church, that, of all the daily services, Matins is the most key and the most central! This hypothesis is strengthened by a passage from St Cyprian of Carthage: "We should pray in the early morning, that, by means of our morning prayer, the Resurrection of the Lord might be recalled."[21] The Eucharist, then, is our experience of the fulness of the Kingdom, given to us now in anticipation, but with its **_full consummation_** taking place at the Parousia! These two complementary functions of the liturgical dualism of eschatology, the "already" and the "not yet," **_must_** be kept in mind and manifested **_liturgically_** in the various services of the Orthodox Church!

---

[21] St Cyprian of Carthage, *De Oratione*, p. 35, quoted in Schmemann, op. cit., p. 82.

3
VESPERS

Even though there are four types of Vespers (Resurrectional, Great, Daily, and Daily Lenten) that are done in parishes, from a liturgical theology standpoint they are all very similar. Therefore, we will treat "Vespers" as a general category, dealing with the specifics of each type as we go along.[22]

A. PSALM 103

If the service is either Daily Vespers or Daily Lenten Vespers, a reader will chant the "Come, Let Us Worship" and Psalm 103.[23] If the service is either Resurrectional Vespers or Great Vespers, these two liturgical elements will be sung by the singers. Sung Vespers developed in the Church in the cathedral rites of parishes, while in monasteries there developed the canon of psalmody. In **both** rites, the basic formative element of worship and their

---

[22] The fifth type, Little Vespers, is specific to monasteries and is almost *never* done in parishes, so it will not be discussed here.

[23] The numbering of the Psalms is according to the Septuagint.

fundamental liturgical source was the Psalter.[24] In the early Church, Vespers began with three units consisting of three Psalms each: Psalm Unit 1 contained Psalms 86, 92 (or 15), and an unknown Psalm; Psalm Unit 2 consisted of Psalms 140, 141, and 129; Psalm Unit 3 was made up of Psalms 114, 115, and 116.[25] Later on, in the 8th and 9th centuries, Psalm 103 came to replace this liturgical "block" of the three units of Psalms, as seen in both the *Horologion* of St Sabbas the Sanctified and the monastic vesperal canon of Abba Nilus of Sinai.[26]

What is important to remember here is that, from the very beginning of the life of the Church, even as she first developed her liturgical life from that of the Old Testament Jewish temple, the Psalter and the singing of psalmody were **essential** and **central** elements in the life of the Church. In later centuries, with the development of elaborate non-Psalter hymnody and sacred song, the use of the Psalter became more minimized in the liturgical life

---

[24] Uspensky, Nicholas D., *Evening Worship in the Orthodox Church*, translated and edited by Paul Lazor, SVS (St Vladimir's Seminary) Press, Crestwood, NY, 1985, (hereafter referred to as "*Evening Worship*"), pp. 58-69.

[25] Ibid, p. 55. In Uspensky's book, the Psalms are numbered according to the Septuagint.

[26] Ibid, p. 69.

of the Church. This is evident today, especially in this vesperal element here, where many of the music books have the chanters singing a reduction of Psalm 103 (what one person called, "the Reader's Digest setting" of the Psalm).

A more ancient, appropriate, and Orthodox restoration of this liturgical element would be to do the entire Psalm 103 in a **responsorial Psalmody** format, with alternating choirs, trios, and the congregation in the nave singing the opening verses of the Psalm, then having a reader chant subsequent Psalm verses interspersed with the people singing the refrain, "Blessed are You, O Lord," or, in a more comfortably grammatical syntax setting, "You are blest, O Lord.". After the entire Psalm has been chanted, the reader can then chant, "Glory to the Father, and to the Son, and to the Holy Spirit!", followed by the people singing, "Glory to You, O Lord, Who have created all!". The reader will then chant, "Now and ever and unto ages of ages! Amen.", followed by the people again singing, "Glory to You, O Lord, Who have created all!". This entire liturgical element will then conclude with the people singing, "Alleluia! Alleluia! Alleluia! Glory to You, O God!", *three* times. The setting composed by Fr Sergei Glagolev follows this pattern *exactly*, and is a good one to use as a guide for future liturgical music composers.

B. LITANIES

All of the litanies of the Church, the Great Litany, the Little Litany, the Augmented Litany, the Litany of Supplication, and the Litany of Thanksgiving, are ***dialogical*** in nature and function. That is, they consist of petitions chanted by the priest or deacon, and are then affirmed (or, better yet, confirmed) by the response of the people in the liturgical assemby. These response are usually "Lord, have mercy," "Grant it, O Lord," "To You, O Lord," "And with your spirit," and "Amen." Being in the form of a liturgical dialogue, it is important that they be done in such a manner that all of the petitions can be clearly heard and understood, with ***no*** overlapping of singing to hide any portion of the petitions, so that the people may intelligently and spiritually fully respond with the appropriate wording of confirmation.

Furthermore, the singing of ***all*** litanies by ***all*** of the people in the congregation should be encouraged and practiced in all parishes. Clergy and choir directors put in much effort to get more lay participation on the part of the liturgical community by encouraging the congregation to join in the singing of the Creed and the Lord's Prayer. However, the most **basic** and **natural** inclusion of the liturgical assembly is involvement of the people in the responses in this liturgical dialogue. This obvious involvement is inherent in the first petition of most of these litanies, which states, "Let **us** pray to the Lord."

Since this dialogical function of litanies precludes the participation of the liturgical assembly, it behooves Church musicians, especially choir directors, to select arrangements and settings of litanies that are easy for the people to sing. This does **not** mean that the arrangements need to be simplistic or boring. It **does**, however, mean that the settings should not be so complex and florid that it resembles an operatic aria. The litany responses should also be directed in a light, brisk manner that avoids the heavy dragging out of half notes and whole notes, which not only distorts the liturgical text of the hymnology but also weighs down the service to a plodding pace. Again, the participation of the "royal priesthood" in the singing of litany responses should be the first line of increased involvement on the part of the liturgical assembly.

C. KATHISMATA

For Resurrectional Vespers on Saturday evening, the 1st Kathisma from the Psalter, Psalms 1-8 (beginning with, "Blessed is the man who walks not in the counsel of the wicked!"), is prescribed to be sung. As mentioned earlier, due to the developing reduction of the use of the Psalter being replaced with elaborate hymnography over the centuries, it is now the practice in many parishes to sing a greatly abridged version of this 1st Kathisma. Again, as was the situation with Psalm 103, it would be appropriate to restore this full 1st Kathisma, either having it sung in its entirety, or to have it done as in the responsorial Psalm format, with chanted verses of the Psalms by a reader being interspersed with a refrain sung by the people.

Concerning the celebration of Great Vespers for feasts on other days of the week, it is ***not*** appropriate to just automatically and unthinkingly insert the singing of the 1st Kathisma at this point. What ***is*** appropriate is to restore the singing of the other Kathismata that are called for at that particular Great Vespers. For example, if there is a Friday feast day with the celebration of Great Vespers on

Thursday evening, the 15th Kathisma, comprising Psalms 105-108, would be sung. This is currently the practice done in monasteries. It would be encouraging and spiritually illuminating if the Kathismata for the other evenings of the week would be set to music and made available for use in parishes.

As for Daily Vespers and Daily Lenten Vespers, at this point, the Kathismata would be chanted by a reader.

D. STIKHERA

The next liturgical element in all forms of Vespers is the singing of "Lord, I Call Upon You" with the accompanying stikhera. Most of the time, there are anywhere from three to ten stikhera sung. Resurrectional Vespers, with no additional material added from other feasts, has seven stikhera. Daily Vespers and Daily Lenten Vespers usually have three stikhera. After the prescribed number of stikhera, there is one final stikheron, either after a full "Glory,...now and ever...!" or after a "'split' Glory" ("Glory...Spirit!", stikheron, "Now and ever...Amen." final stikheron).

A word of caution needs to be enumerated here. In many parishes, where the choir director wants to call attention to himself or herself and the musical prowess of their particular choir, there is a tendency to "pile on" additional stikhera for minor saints in the Church calendar that almost no one has heard of, just to augment the singing element of the services. This applies to the stikhera for the Apostikha as well as those for "Lord, I Call Upon You." What all choir directors should keep in mind is that the main liturgical celebrant for that particular service, be it the parish priest, the diocesan bishop, or the metropolitan, is the person who decides the specifics of that service for the day, whether it be in cutting back a Little Litany, adding or deleting stikhera, etc. The choir director should consult the main celebrant ahead of time, to put into place the liturgical directives for that day, so that, in the words of St Paul, everything "should be done decently and in order" (1 Cor 14:40).

One final point: Both the "Lord, I Call Upon You" stikhera and the stikhera for the Apostikha serve as sort of "bookends" as beginning and ending stikhera for Vespers, respectively. Therefore, to manifest this connection, it is appropriate to sing both sets of stikhera, for "Lord, I Call Upon You" and the Apostikha, in the same musical setting, whether it be Byzantine Chant, Kievan Chant, etc.

E. "GLADSOME LIGHT"

We now come to the central element and, therefore, hymn of Vespers, "Gladsome Light." In the time of the Jerusalem Church, a burning lamp was brought into the church from within the building itself, that is, from the cave of the Lord's own tomb.[27] This was a double manifestation, first of Christ as the Light of the world, and also of Him as the One Who arose from the dead. This ritual of the burning lamp was a continuation of the practice of the Old Testament Israelites, who were commanded by God to keep a lamp burning outside the veil of the testimony, in the tent of meeting (Lev 24:1-4).[28] This procession with the burning lamp is preserved in the Liturgy of the Presanctified Gifts, whereby the priest comes out of the sanctuary after the Second Prokeimenon and proclaims, while holding a burning candle, "The Light of Christ illumines all!"[29] In the

---

[27] *Evening Worship*, pp. 30-31.
[28] Ibid, p. 14.
[29] Ibid, p. 31.

ancient Church, at Vespers, the clergy chanted several Prayers of Light.[30] This clearly illustrates the vesperal theme of Christ as the Light of the world.

This theme of Christ as the Light is very scriptural, being a central focal point of the Gospel according to St John the Theologian. Along with Christ as the Light being the nexus of the Prologue of the Gospel (Jn 1:4-9), other Johannine passages manifest this as well: "I Am the Light of the world! He who follows Me will not walk in darkness, but will have the light of life!" (Jn 8:12); "As long as I am in the world, I Am the Light of the world!" (Jn 9:5); and "He who sees Me sees Him Who sent Me! I have come as Light into the world, that whoever believes in Me may not remain in darkness!" (Jn 12:45-46).[31] This is also shown in the First Epistle of John in some passages (1 Jn 1:5-7; 2:8-11).[32] The great liturgical scholar, Robert F. Taft, SJ, acknowledges the centrality of this theme to Vespers: "[After the first basic element of the sanctification of time,] (t)his is the second basic element of the rite of (V)espers in every tradition: thanksgiving for the light, in which the Church uses the lamplighting at sunset to remind

---

[30] Ibid, pp. 44-54.
[31] *Beyond East and West*, p. 173.
[32] Ibid, p. 174.

us of the Johannine vision of the Lamb (W)ho is the eternal (L)amp of the Heavenly Jerusalem, the (S)un (T)hat never sets."[33]

    Thus, "Gladsome Light" still forms the core of the light service of Byzantine Vespers.[34] As such, the singing of it at Resurrectional, Great, and Daily Vespers, and the chanting of it by a reader at Daily Lenten Vespers, should be done in a solemn manner, befitting the centrality of this liturgical element. Musical settings that are elaborate, yet prayful enough so that the music does not detract from the text, are to be encouraged. Also, before the singing of the hymn and the entrance, once the clergy and servers have exited the sanctuary to the center of the church, it is encouraged to have the main celebrant chant the Prayer of Light, that begins, "In the evening, in the morning, and at noonday,....!", in order to liturgically emphasize this central theme of light in Vespers.

---

[33] Ibid, p. 180.
[34] Ibid, p. 179.

F. THE EVENING PROKEIMENON

Today, the modern practice of the Prokeimenon in liturgical services consists of one verse from a Psalm chanted by a reader and then sung by the people; the reader chanting a response verse from the same Psalm and the people repeating the singing of the first verse; the reader then chanting the first half of the first verse, with the people responding with the second half of the first verse.

In the early Church, the celebration of the **full** Psalm in its **entirety** was the norm. The key clue to this is that, in the modern practice, the second verse for **each** Prokeimenon is **the <u>first</u> verse of the Psalm being celebrated**, <u>unless</u> **the refrain is from the first verse**. In **that** case, the response verse would be from the <u>**second**</u> verse of the Psalm. This is true for the Prokeimenon for every day of the week:

Saturday evening: "The Lord is King! He is robed in majesty!" (Psalm 93:1) has, for the response verse, "For, He has established the world, so that it will never be moved!" (Psalm 93:1).

Sunday evening: "Come, bless the Lord, all you servants of the Lord!" (Psalm 133:1) [the Antiochians have, from the same Psalm, "You who stand in the temple of the Lord, in the courts of the house of our God!" (Psalm 133:1)], has, for the response verse, "Lift up your hands to the holy place, and bless the Lord!" (Psalm 133:2).

Monday evening: "The Lord hears when I call to Him!" (Psalm 4:3) has, for the response verse, "Answer me when I call, God of my right! You have given me room when I was in distress! Be gracious to me, and hear my prayer!" (Psalm 4:1).

Tuesday evening: "Your mercy, O Lord, will follow me all the days of my life!" (Psalm 22:6) has, for the response verse, "The Lord is my Shepherd! I will not want! He makes me lie down in green pastures!" (Psalm 22:1).

Wednesday evening: "Save me, O God, by Your Name, and judge me by Your strength!" (Psalm 53:1) has, for the response verse, "Hear my prayer, O God! Give ear to the words of my mouth!" (Psalm 53:2).

Thursday evening: "My help comes from the Lord, Who made Heaven and Earth!" (Psalm 120:2) has, for the response verse, "I lift up my eyes to the hills! From where does my help come?" (Psalm 120:1).

Friday evening: "You, O God, are my Helper, and Your steadfast love will go before me!" (Psalm 58:9-10) has, for the response verse, "Deliver me from my enemies, O God! Protect me from those who rise up against me!" (Psalm 58:1).

Once again, it would be appropriate to restore the practice of the Prokeimenon to the ancient ordo of celebrating **the Psalm _in_ _its_ _entirety!_** Ironically, many parishes are actually doing this in the Divine Liturgy when the clergy are receiving Holy Communion: the reader of the day chants each of the Psalm verses, interspersed with the people singing the refrain verse of the Prokeimenon Psalm. The authentic Orthodox practice would be to sing this fuller version at the time of the service of the Prokeimenon itself.

G. OLD / NEW TESTAMENT READINGS

On feast days that call for readings from the Old or the New Testaments, these readings would be chanted at this point. There would be three separate readings done. The usual parish custom is to have three separate readers doing the readings, usually from the center of the nave.

The chanting of Scripture readings is a very ancient liturgical element of the Church. Being such a central component of the services, the preparation for such readings should not be taken lightly. Competent and well-trained readers need to this ministry **very** seriously. Those readers who have quality experience should be considered for the more difficult readings, those with hard-to-pronounce proper names. In most parishes, it is usually the choir director who is given the task of training and overseeing the ministry of the readers in the community. Open communication and full disclosure of situations with the parish priest will ensure that this ministry is celebrated in the manner befitting respect and reverence of the Holy Scriptures.

H. MATINS GOSPEL

If either Saturday evening Resurrectional Vespers or a weekday Great Vespers is not followed by either Resurrectional or Festal Matins, it is both appropriate and encouraged for the parish to do the Resurrectional or Festal Matins Gospel at this time. The Matins Gospel is essential and central to the celebration of the Lord's Day and feasts of the Church, and it is spiritually fulfilling for the faithful to liturgically experience this Gospel reading at the Vespers service, if no Matins is to follow.

I. LITYA AND RESPONSES

If there is a feast, either on a Sunday coinciding with Resurrectional Vespers or during the week with the celebration of Great Vespers, Litya verses are sung and followed by litany petitions chanted by the clergy. In some parishes, there is an *abbreviated* version done, consisting of *four* petitions: the people sing "Lord, have mercy." *twelve* times after each of the first two petitions and *three* times after each of the second two petitions.

However, the **fuller** version, which **should** be **restored** in parishes, consists of **five** petitions. After the first **three** petitions, the people respond with "Lord, have mercy." sung **twelve** times. After the next **two** petitions, the people respond with "Lord, have mercy." sung **three** times.

Being a festive liturgical element, the Litya verses and the litany responses that follow should be done in a brisk, bright, joyful manner, with both the festal stikhera and petition responses sung in a clearly articulated manner.

J. CONCLUDING TROPARIA

There are many and varied patterns and combinations of the troparia that conclude Vespers, depending on whether it is the Lord's Day, a feast day, a regular weekday, or a day during Great Lent.[35] Two points need to be mentioned here. The first one is that the practice should be whatever one is in

---

[35] Cf. the specifics on the patterns and combinations of these troparia in my book, *Liturgics for Orthodox Liturgical Singing • Volume 1*, OLP (Orthodox Liturgical Press), Southbury, CT, July 2015, Chapter 1, "Vespers," pp. 1-76.

place in the local parish, as determined by the main celebrant of the service, be he the parish priest, diocesan bishop, etc. The second point is one made earlier when discussing the stikhera on "Lord, I Call Upon You": In many parishes, where the choir director wants to call attention to himself or herself and the musical prowess of their particular choir, there is a tendency to "pile on" additional troparia for minor saints in the Church calendar that almost no one has heard of, just to augment the singing element of the services. This practice should be discouraged, keeping the troparia reserved for the particular feast day, the patron saint of that parish community, and major saints of the Church.

K.   PARISH VIGIL: A PROPOSED ORDO

Generally speaking, whenever both Vespers and Matins are called for, whether for the Sunday services for the Resurrection of Christ on the Lord's Day or for a feast of the Church during the midst of the week, there are two styles of celebrating these services. The Byzantines serve Vespers on the evening of the feast and Matins on the morning of the feast, before the Divine Liturgy. The Slavs tend to combine both Vespers and Matins together on the eve of the feast in what is known as a Vigil service. Originally called the "All-Night Vigil" because, when done in its full form, complete with all the liturgical elements called for (as would be more fully done in a monastery), the service would literally take all night to celebrate. Naturally, this would be anything but practical for life in a parish. Fortunately, a proposal was made some years ago by Dr Paul Meyendorff, Professor of Liturgical Theology at St Vladimir's Orthodox Theological Seminary. In an article published in the newsletter of the Diocese of New York and New Jersey of the Orthodox Church in America, *Jacob's Well*, Dr Meyendorff proposed an ordo for a parish Vigil service that is both doable and meaningful.[36] This ordo, with quotes from the footnoted article, is as follows.

"Few people today would argue for a return to the monastic practice of celebrating an eight-hour Vigil each Saturday night. Even the greatly

---

[36] Meyendorff, Dr. Paul, "Saturday Evening Worship: A Proposal", *Jacob's Well*, Newsletter of the Diocese of New York and New Jersey, Orthodox Church in America, Spring 1995 issue, p. 5. I have recently had confirmed by Dr Meyendorff himself that his proposed ordo presented here in my book is accurate and exact as he himself presented it.

abbreviated two-hour Vigil, so popular in 19th-century Russia, survives only in our seminaries and in a tiny minority of parishes. The 'typical' parish today celebrates only Great Vespers, which typically lasts from 30-45 minutes and is attended by 10-25% of the parishioners. Many clergy and faithful who attend this brief service have expressed a desire for something more. On the one hand, parishioners who may drive a half-hour or more to get to church feel that this service is too brief: why make all the effort to get ready and come to church for such a brief service? On the other hand, clergy who have, if only in their seminary training experienced a fuller liturgical cycle, realize that the faithful never hear the Sunday Resurrection Gospel proclaimed, except once a year on Holy Saturday! This Gospel, located in the middle of Matins, is the focal point of the weekly Resurrection Vigil and certainly ought to be restored."

Basically, the proposed ordo for the parish Vigil would encompass the following elements (some of these, as designated, are applicable only for a Resurrectional Vigil for Saturday evenings, while others are appropriate only for a Festal Vigil celebrated for Church feast days during the week:[37]

1) Resurrectional or Great Vespers, in its entirety, up to right before the Dismissal.
2) Psalm 118 or the Polyeleos (Psalms 135-136).
3) Psalm 137 ("By the Waters of Babylon"), during Great Lent only.
4) Megalynarion, for Festal Vigil on feast days only.
5) Evlogitaria ("Blessed are You, O Lord! Teach me Your statutes!"), for Resurrectional Vigil only.
6) Hymns of Degrees, "From My Youth", for Festal Vigil on feast days only.
7) Matins Prokeimenon and "Let Every Breath".
8) Resurrectional or Festal Matins Gospel.
9) Resurrectional troparia ("Having Beheld the Resurrection of Christ"), for Resurrectional Vigil only.

---

[37] The liturgical theology aspects of the specifics of Matins itself will be covered in the following chapter.

10) **Vesperal** Dismissal.

As Dr Meyendorff stated in his article, "Remarkably, this proposed service is also very much a return to ancient practice. For 700-800 years, in the cathedral of Constantinople, Hagia Sophia, the Saturday evening service was very much like this, consisting of Vespers and a brief service called a *pannychis* (= Vigil). It contained much singing, processions, incensations; and all the people sang the responses to the psalmody. This can still be seen in the refrains at the Polyeleos and the Evlogitaria, and there is no reason why these should not be sung by the entire congregation."

From a liturgical theology perspective, such a service would be liturgically and spiritually nourishing to serious Orthodox Christians, and, again, is very practical and doable in the context of a parish setting.

4
MATINS

The celebration of Matins has fallen into disuse in the liturgical life of the Church, especially in parishes. This is unfortunate, because many of the matinal elements are key liturgical essentials for manifesting the meaning of the feasts in our Church. One such example, as we will see, is the Matins Gospel.

Just as with Vespers, even though there are four types of Matins (Resurrectional, Festal, Daily, and Daily Lenten) that are done in parishes, from a liturgical theology standpoint they are all very similar. Therefore, we will treat "Matins" as a general category, dealing with the specifics of each type as we go along.

A. THE SIX PSALMS

A reader then chants the Six Psalms of Matins, Psalms 3, 37, 62, 87, 102, and 143. It is customary in many parishes to have **two** readers chant the Six Psalms, each reader chanting three of the Psalms. In some parishes, the practice is to read only one, two, or three of the Psalms. The reason usually given for that is to not make the Matins service seem exceedingly long. While keeping the length of the service to a pastorally doable length is a viable concern, it seems that other places in the service would make better choices for cutting back. The chanting of the Psalter goes back to the Old Testament times of ancient Israel. These six particular Psalms, a fixed feature of Matins, all comprise the theme of the morning, of the early part of the day as appropriate to give thanks, praise, and glory to God. It would be more fitting to cut back (or, even, cut out) one of the litanies, such as the Litany of Supplication, or to take fewer Kathisma Hymns in the service. In other words, it is more essential to celebrate the reading of actual Scripture than it is to sing commentaries on it.

B. LITANIES

As mentioned in our discussion of Vespers, **all** of the litanies of the Church, the Great Litany, the Little Litany, the Augmented Litany, the Litany of Supplication, and the Litany of Thanksgiving, are ***dialogical*** in nature and function. Again, the participation of the "royal priesthood" in the singing of litany responses should be the first line of increased involvement on the part of the liturgical assembly.

C. "GOD IS THE LORD" OR "ALLELUIA!" AND TROPARIA

The singing of "God is the Lord" (for all seasons except Great Lent) or "Alleluia!" (for Great Lent only) and the troparion or troparia for the day is then sung. The singing of "God is the Lord" is interspersed with verses Psalm 117; the singing if "Alleluia!" is interspersed with verses from Isaiah 26. This, also, is a fixed liturgical element of Matins. "God is the Lord" is a positive affirmation of God's divinity and a statement of praise to the Son of God ("Blessed is He Who comes in the Name of the Lord!"). Therefore, it should be sung in a spirit and a manner of joyful affirmation. This is even true for the singing of the "Alleluia!" during Great Lent. Furthermore, it is important that the singing of "God is the Lord" or "Alleluia!" be done so that the interspersed verses from Psalm 117 or Isaiah 26 are **not** covered over or overlapped with the singing.

Once the interspersed verse is fully chanted, **then** the singing of the refrain should resume.

D. KATHISMATA AND THE POLYELEOS

The next liturgical "block" of elements is comprised of Kathisma (readings from the Psalter), Kathisma Hymns, and possibly, depending on the type of Matins, the Polyeleos.

All forms of Matins include the Kathisma and Kathisma Hymns. Again, readings from the Psalter are included in the most ancient types of worship and should **not** be eliminated or cut back. The singing of the Kathisma Hymns, however, being **commentaries** on the Psalm readings, **may** be reduced to just one or two of the hymns, for the reason previously stated, namely, the pastoral concern for the length of the service.

The Polyeleos is prescribed to be sung on all Sundays and feast days (that is, for Resurrectional and Festal Matins) from the Leavetaking of the Exaltation of the Holy Cross (22 September) through Forgiveness (Cheesefare) Sunday. However, in parish practice, the Polyeleos is usually sung all year round. Also, the Polyleos is such an essential feature of Matins that Dr Paul Meyendorff included it in his proposed ordo for a parish Vigil.[38] In the article from ***Jacob's Well*** that proposed this ordo, Dr Meyendorff said, "Remarkably, this proposed service is also very much a return to ancient practice. For 700-800 years, in the cathedral of Constantinople, Hagia Sophia, the Saturday evening service was very much like this, consisting of Vespers and a brief service called a ***pannychis*** (= Vigil). It contained much singing, processions, incensations; and all the people sang the responses to the psalmody. This can still be seen in the refrains at the Polyeleos and the Evlogitaria, and there is no reason why these should not be sung by the entire congregation."[39] This style of singing, incorporating Psalm verses with an interspersed refrain, is one of the oldest styles of hymnody in the Orthodox Church, and should ***definitely be <u>restored</u>*** in our liturgical services wherever appropriate and possible.

---

[38] See above, pp.54-58.
[39] Meyendorff, Dr Paul, *Jacob's Well*, op. cit., p. 5.

E. PSALM 137 AND THE MEGALYNARION

The singing of Psalm 137, "By the Waters of Babylon," is done *only* during Great Lent. Therefore, it should be sung in a quiet, solemn, penitential manner. Being an important element of Great Lent, it is also, as we saw in the last chapter, an integral part of the proposed parish Vigil.

Another element included in that proposed Vigil is the Megalynarion, or Magnification. This is sung (in the Slavic tradition) or chanted by a reader (in the Byzantine practice, utilizing the Psalm verses only) at Festal Matins for different feasts of the Church. Since this is sung or chanted at the same time as a great censing of the church building is done, it is usually done, after the initial chanting of the Megalynarion once by the clergy, it is then sung or chanted three times, with "Glory...Spirit!" chanted by a reader after the first time and "Now and ever...Amen." after the second time. Also, each time it should be done slowly and reverently, to give the clergy enough time to complete the great censing of the church building.

F. EVLOGITARIA, HYPAKOE, AND HYMNS OF DEGREES

Also included in the proposed Vigil is the singing of the Evlogitaria, "Blessed are You, O Lord! Teach me Your statutes!", called for on Sundays during Resurrectional Matins only. Being an element, therefore, of **Resurrectional** Matins, it should be sung in a joyous, festal manner. As with the Megalynarion, the Evlogitaria is done during a great censing of the church building. However, being a long hymn with extended text, it does **not** need to be done slowly or repeatedly. Singing it through once, even at a brisk, festal pace, will still provide enough time for the great censing to be completed. Also, as with the Polyeleos, the singing of the repeated refrain of the Evlogitaria ("Blessed are You, O Lord! Teach me Your statutes!") all of the congregation should ***definitely be restored***.

The Hypakoe is a troparion (in the tone of the week) in preparation for the Resurrectional Matins Gospel, emphasizing the discovery of the empty tomb by the myrrh-bearing women. This liturgical element is **not** included in the proposed parish Vigil. Therefore, it **is** an element that may be omitted from

Resurrectional Matins if the time constraint of the service is of pastoral concern.

The final element in this liturgical "block" is the singing of the First Antiphon of the Hymn of Degrees, beginning with the words, "From my youth". This is called for on Church feast days at Festal Matins only. It *is* included in the proposed parish Vigil, and everyone present at the service should be encouraged to sing it.

G.   PROKEIMENA

At both Resurrectional and Festal Matins, Prokeimena are chanted, followed by the Matins Gospel for the day. First, there is the Prokeimenon for the day, followed by an exclamation, then the fixed Prokeimenon for Matins, "Let every breath praise the Lord!".

What we said in the last chapter, concerning the Prokeimenon for Vespers, applies here as well.[40] Once again, it would be appropriate to restore the practice of the Prokeimenon to the ancient ordo of

---

[40] See above, pp. 40-43.

celebrating **the Psalm *in its* entirety!** The authentic Orthodox practice would be to sing this fuller version of the Prokeimenon. Furthermore, it should be sung clearly and solemnly, with **no** overlapping of singing covering up the Psalm verses.

H. MATINS GOSPEL

The Prokeimena are followed by the Matins Gospel. What is apparent when one looks closely at the Scripture readings for the feasts throughout the Church year is that the **Matins** Gospel reading is, more often than not, the more **central** reading than the one for the Divine Liturgy. This is made more obvious by the liturgical rule that the Divine Liturgy Gospel reading may be chanted by a bishop, a priest, or a deacon, **but** the **Matins** Gospel reading may be chanted **only** by a bishop or a priest, but **not** a deacon! Another liturgical "sign" of this is the fact that, while the Divine Liturgy Gospel may be chanted by a deacon in the center of the nave, the Matins Gospel is **always** chanted by the bishop or the priest from the **altar** itself. This centrality of Matins for a feast day applies not only to the Gospel reading, but also for the full inclusion of the three services,

Vespers, Matins, and the Divine Liturgy, themselves. Vespers begins the presentation of the festal elements, Matins then develops them more fully, and then the Divine Liturgy is somewhat more placid liturgically from the standpoint of the **development** of the festal elements. Therefore, one **could** say that if someone wanted to pick one service to see what the Church fully has to say about a particular feast, they should look to Matins.

I. "HAVING BEHELD THE RESURRECTION OF CHRIST", PSALM 50, AND TROPARION

The next liturgical "block" of elements consists of "Having Beheld the Resurrection of Christ," Psalm 50, and the Troparion.

"Having Beheld the Resurrection of Christ" is the post-Gospel Resurrection Troparion sung **only** at Resurrectional Matins. Being the **Resurrection** Troparion, it should be sung in a joyous and festive manner. Also, to further this festive character of the hymn, if one were to err on the side of caution, it would preferable to pitch this hymn for the singers in a higher key rather than a lower one, to manifest the "brightness" of the hymn itself.

Psalm 50 is a fixed staple in all four types of Matins (Resurrectional, Festal, Daily, and Daily Lenten) that are celebrated in parishes. In the Byzantine practice, Psalm 50 is sung antiphonally in tone 6 for both Resurrectional and Festal Matins. In the Slavic tradition, it is chanted by a reader for all types of Matins. Whichever the practice, this Psalm is one of the most central ones of the Church and the one used most frequently liturgically, being the first one chanted at the 3rd Hour, as well as being found in Grand Compline during Great Lent and verses of it being chanted by the clergy right before the consecration of the Holy Gifts at the Divine Liturgy. Therefore, it should be done in a clearly articulated and solemn manner.

For Festal Matins only, the festal Troparion of the feast is then sung by the people.

J. THE KANON

The Kanon is a structured hymn, consisting of nine **odes**, sometimes called **canticles** or **songs** depending on the translation, based on the Biblical canticles. Most of these are found in the Old Testament, but the final ode is taken from the Magnificat and the Song of Zechariah in the New Testament. Over time the Kanon (coming from Palestinian monastic usage) came to replace the Kontakion (which grew out of the cathedral practice of Constantinople), a form of which is still used on several occasions and that has been incorporated into the performance of the Kanon (after the 6th ode).

Being a structured hymn rather than psalmody, the Kanon can be pared down somewhat by taking only one or two troparia after the heirmos. You can either take the first troparion, then the "Glory...now and ever..." and then the final troparion; or, after the heirmos, just take the "Glory...now and ever..." and then the final troparion.

K. THE EXAPOSTILARION

The Exapostilarion is a hymn that is preparatory for the Praises and the Doxology that follows it. The Exapostilarion for both the Matins of

Holy Friday and Pascha are very central to the service. This Hymn of Light should be done quite reverently.

L. THE PRAISES

The Praises are then done. At both Resurrectional and Festal Matins, they are sung and also have accompanying stikhera. At both Daily and Daily Lenten Matins, they are chanted by a reader with**out** any stikhera accompanying them (in the Greek practice, the Praises are omitted at Daily Lenten Matins only). The intent is that the Praises will be chanted as the sun begins to arise. Being taken from the concluding three Psalms of the Psalter (Psalms 148, 149, and 150), they are joyful commands to all of creation to praise the Lord. Therefore, they should be done in a joyful, uplifting manner.

M. THE DOXOLOGY

The Doxology is an ancient hymn of praise to the Trinity that is sung or chanted daily. In Resurrectional and Festal Matins, it is called the Great Doxology, is sung, and concludes with the Trisagion. For Daily and Daily Lenten Matins, it is called the Lesser Doxology, is chanted by a reader, and does **not** conclude with the Trisagion. It begins with the exclamation, "Glory to You, Who have shone us the Light!". In monasteries, the time for the beginning of Matins is scheduled so that, hopefully, this exclamation of the Doxology occurs simultaneously with the sun first shining into the windows of the church building. As such, it makes the Doxology to be the culmination element of Matins. Therefore, it should **always** be celebrated and **never** abbreviated. Being a hymn of praise, it should be done, as were the Praises, in a joyful, uplifting manner.

N. THE LITURGICAL CENTRALITY OF MATINS

As discussed earlier, both here and in the aforementioned article by Dr Paul Meyendorff, Matins has always occupied a central in the liturgical life of the Orthodox Church. Again, many of the paschal elements for Sunday and the festal elements for feast days are found in Resurrectional and Festal Matins, respectively. Festal Matins, especially, contains the Gospel reading for the feast that is often more central than the one found in the Divine Liturgy. The proposed parish Vigil offered by Dr Meyendorff for Sundays and feast days should be very seriously considered. Matins is also the foundational "ordo" of such non-sacramental services as Thanksgiving (Molieben) and Memorial (Panakhida).

More and more parishes are now expanding their liturgical ordo by celebrating the weekday services of Daily Vespers and Daily Matins. Those faithful Orthodox who are able to attend such services, be they retirees, housewives, self-employed parishioners, or those working from home, are discovering the spiritually nourishing benefits from the liturgical rhythm of the daily services. Some of these parishes celebrate each service daily. Others alternate the services in any of numerous combinations, such as Daily Matins on Mondays, Wednesdays, and Fridays, and Daily Vespers on Tuesdays and Thursdays. Whatever combination and frequency of services is most appropriate for the specific needs of the local parish community, the increased rhythm of celebrating the daily services should be encouraged.

5
THE DIVINE LITURGY

Essentially, the Divine Liturgy is a two-course banquet: First, we are nourished on the readings from Scripture (the Epistle and the Gospel); second, we are fed on the Body and Blood of Christ in the Eucharist! The proof of this is that these are precisely the two things that are processed in the two liturgical entrances, the Gospel Book and the Holy Gifts. It is also the Sacrament of the Kingdom of God, and, especially, of the **resurrected** Christ! As such, **everything** chanted or sung in the Divine Liturgy should be done in a joyous, resurrectional, and eschatological manner!

A. DOXOLOGY

The doxology for **_all_** Divine Liturgies is, "Blessed is the Kingdom of the Father, and of the Son, and of the Holy Spirit, now and ever and unto ages of ages!" This reveals the **eschatological** centrality of the Divine Liturgy, which is why Fr Alexander Schmemann included for his book, **The Eucharist**, the subtitle. **The Sacrament of the**

Kingdom.[41] As stated above, ***everything*** for the Divine Liturgy should be sung in a joyous, resurrectional, and eschatological manner, ***especially*** the "Amen" that is the response on the part of the people to the opening doxology!

B. LITANIES

As mentioned in the previous two chapters, ***all*** of the litanies of the Church, the Great Litany, the Little Litany, the Augmented Litany, the Litany of Supplication, and the Litany of Thanksgiving, are ***dialogical*** in nature and function. Again, the participation of the "royal priesthood" in the singing of litany responses should be the first line of increased involvement on the part of the liturgical assembly.

---

[41] Schmemann, Alexander, *The Eucharist: Sacrament of the Kingdom*, SVS Press, Crestwood, NY, 1988 (hereafter referred to as, "*Eucharist*").

C. THE ANTIPHONS

The singing of the First, Second, and Third Antiphons at the Divine Liturgy consists of one entire "block" of liturgical elements. Therefore, in order to manifest this connection of liturgical unification, it is encouraged that the same musical setting be used in the singing of all three antiphons.

In the early Church, the antiphons were sung in the procession of the liturgical assembly on its way to the specific church where the Divine Liturgy was to be celebrated that day.[42] The function, therefore, of the antiphons was to accompany **liturgical movement**. The more ancient practice for the celebration of the antiphons at the Divine Liturgy, then, was to do them in the **Psalm antiphon** format, with alternating choirs, trios, and the congregation in the nave singing the opening verses of the Psalm (here, for the First Antiphon, it is Psalm 102), then having a reader chant subsequent Psalm verses interspersed with the people singing the refrain, "Blessed are You, O Lord!", or, in a more comfortably grammatical syntax setting, "You are blest, O Lord!". Setting these antiphons in this

---

[42] Taft, *Beyond East and West*, pp. 210-211.

format would be relatively easy for talented Orthodox liturgical musicians who have these skills, and the incorporation of this liturgical participation on the part of all the faithful present would require a minimum of preparation and transition. This style of singing and involvement of all those present should **definitely be <u>restored</u>** in the Divine Liturgy.

D. THE THIRD ANTIPHON

At *most* Divine Liturgies throughout the year, the Third Antiphon consists in the singing of the Beatitudes. Once again, the restoration of singing the Beatitudes in the Psalm antiphon format should be restored. Actually, it *is* celebrated that way during Holy Week, at the Matins of Holy Friday, between the 6th and the 7th Passion Gospels. There, the first few verses of the Beatitudes are sung; then, the deacon begins chanting a series of verses, in between which the people continue singing the remaining verses of the Beatitudes. At the Divine Liturgy, this chanting of verses can be done by a lay reader. Since the Beatitudes are done at most of the Divine Liturgies celebrated throughout the liturgical year, they are totally familiar to all the people.

Therefore, the singing of it on the part of **all** the faithful present should be encouraged and restored.

For the various feasts of the Lord throughout the year (Christmas, Theophany, etc.), the Third Antiphon consists of Psalm verses chanted by a reader, with the festal troparion sung in between the Psalm verses. During this time, the clergy and servers exit the sanctuary for the Gospel Entrance. When they are all in the center of the church, the deacon raises the Gospel Book, exclaims, "Wisdom! Let us be attentive!", and then chants the Little Introit for the feast. The festal troparion is then sung one final time. Once again, the singing of the festal troparion as the response in this Psalm antiphon format should be restored to the ancient practice of having **all** the faithful present participating in the singing.

E. "COME, LET US WORSHIP"

Most of the time, "Come, Let Us Worship" *is* sung as the entrance hymn for the Gospel Entrance at the Divine Liturgy. The exception to this is for a feast of the Lord, where the Beatitudes at the Third Antiphon are replaced with the singing of the festal troparion interspersed with Psalm verses. In *that* case, once the deacon chants the Little Introit, the people sing the festal troparion one last time *as the clergy and servers enter the sanctuary to complete the entrance*. Then, a full "Glory,…now and ever…" is sung, followed by the festal kontakion. When "Come, Let Us Worship" *is* sung at a regular Divine Liturgy, it should be sung in a joyful, affirmative manner, reflecting the victorious character of the text of the hymn.

At a Hierarchical Divine Liturgy, the standard way to sing "Come, Let Us Worship" the *clergy* begin the singing of "Come, Let Us Worship," with the appropriate insertion and the "Alleluia!" This is followed by the people singing it, but *not* starting at the "Come, Let Us Worship," but *at the insertion* ("Who arose from the dead," etc.) and the "Alleluia!" While the people are singing this, the bishop, clergy, and servers enter the sanctuary. When the people finish singing, the clergy *again* sing, but in the manner just chanted by the people, that is, beginning with the insertion and then the "Alleluia!". What is important here is that the "old style" of the people singing at the same time as the clergy and covering it over (or, out shouting them) should *definitely* be discouraged and eliminated. The proper way to sing this is for the people to wait for the **_clergy to finish_** singing the "Alleluia!" and **_then_** to begin singing at their insertion ("Who arose from the dead," etc.) and the "Alleluia!". Once the **_people have completed_** their singing of "Alleluia!", **_then_** the clergy (now in the sanctuary) sing beginning at their insertion ("Who arose from the dead," etc.) and the "Alleluia!". In this manner, the entire singing of "Come, Let Us Worship" is done in a manner, as St Paul commanded us, "decently and in order." (1 Cor 14:40).

F. TROPARIA AND KONTAKIA

The troparia and kontakia of the day are immediately sung immediately preceding the Trisagion. While a very rushed style of singing, whereby the text of the hymns is unintelligible, is to be avoided, nevertheless, the singing of the troparia and kontakia **_should_** be sung in a brisk, joyful manner.

G. THE TRISAGION

In one sense, all that has gone on in the Divine Liturgy up until now has been preparatory. In the early Church, during the time of intense persecution of Christians, the holy items needed for the service (the Gospel Book, the Holy Gifts, etc.) were kept outside the church building and then brought there in a procession, during which the previous hymns (the antiphons, etc.) were sung, followed by the Gospel Entrance (which was the original beginning of the Divine Liturgy, hence the entrance prayer, "Blessed is the entrance of Your saints!") and the thematic hymns of the day (the troparia and kontakia). Originally, it was the conclusion of the introit antiphon that was sung when, having reached the church building at the end of the liturgical procession, everyone actually entered the church building.[43] At this point, the Divine Liturgy proper, the "meat-and-potatoes" of the service, so to speak, begins, and it begins with this victory hymn acknowledging our God in the Holy Trinity: the Father ("Holy God!"), and the Son ("Holy Mighty!"), and the Holy Spirit ("Holy Immortal!"). That is why

---

[43] Ibid, p. 216.

this hymn is called **the Trisagion**, because the word means "the thrice holy" (from the Greek word "agios" ["*άγιος*"], meaning, "holy").

Therefore, the singing of the Trisagion (be it, "Holy God!", "Before Your Cross!", or "As Many as Have Been Baptized!") should be done in the most joyous, affirming, robust, and victorious manner possible. As with the Gospel reading, the Anaphora, and the Lord's Prayer, **everyone** should stand during the singing of the Trisagion.

H. THE PROKEIMENON

As stated in the earlier chapters in our discussion of both Vespers[44] and Matins,[45] in the early Church, the celebration of the **full** Psalm in its **entirety** was the norm. Once again, it would be appropriate to restore the practice of the Prokeimenon to the ancient ordo of celebrating **the Psalm _in_ _its_ _entirety_**: The reader of the day chants each of the Psalm verses, interspersed with the people singing the refrain verse of the Prokeimenon

---

[44] Cf. above, pp. 40-43.
[45] Cf. above, pp. 69-70.

Psalm. The Prokeimenon would then conclude in the same manner it does nowadays in its abridged version: The reader chants the first half of the refrain verse, and the people sing the second half of the refrain verse. Since the word "prokeimenon" comes from the Greek and means, "that which precedes," its function is to precede or ***introduce*** the reading from the Epistle.[46] The readings from Scripture (the Epistle and the Gospel) comprise the "first course" of the Eucharistic Banquet. ***Therefore***, these readings, along with the liturgical elements that introduce them (such as the Prokeimenon) ***should*** be done in their entirety, at a brisk pace in order not to weigh down the rhythm of the service. The restoration of this practice would more clearly manifest the centrality of the Scripture readings in the Divine Liturgy.

I. THE EPISTLE

As we have just stated, the Scripture readings comprise the "first course" of the Eucharistic Banquet. It is therefore ***imperative*** that they be

---

[46] *Eucharist*, pp. 72-73.

chanted in a **_very_** clear, concise, assertive, and articulately understandable manner! In many (if not most) parishes, the Epistle reading is chanted by a lay man or woman. Thus, it is **_extremely_** important that this person be sufficiently trained so that he or she may proclaim the reading clearly, both for the edification of the faithful and to the glory of God! Along with this, it is a mandatory element of this **_ministry_** of Scriptural chanting that the reader examine, peruse, and practice the reading **_ahead of time!_** Besides looking the reading over so that the complete sentences of the text are understandable, many of the readings contain names of people and places that are difficult to pronounce when closely examined and all but impossible to pronounce when they are sight-read on the spur of the moment. If the reader is unsure on the correct pronunciation of a word in the text, he or she can check with either the choir director or, better yet, the pastor of the parish, who should be more than happy to assist the reader in the correct articulation of the text.

One final comment regarding the Epistle reading: Since the function of the Prokeimenon is to introduce the Epistle reading, the two liturgical elements should agree in number. If a certain feast day calls for two Epistle readings, two Prokeimena should be done. It makes **_no_** sense to have either one Prokeimenon and two Epistle readings, or two Prokeimena and one Epistle reading. Here, the open lines of communication between the choir director (who is usually the person in charge of guiding the parish readers) and the pastor are essential. Discussing these elements clearly ahead of time (will there be one Prokeimenon and one Epistle reading, or two Prokeimena and two Epistle readings?) will eliminate liturgical confusion and the mutation of liturgical practices.

J. "ALLELUIA" VERSES

Just as the Prokeimenon introduces the Epistle reading, so the "Alleluia" Verses introduce the Gospel reading.[47] ***Therefore***, once again, the restoration of ***celebrating the Psalm in its entirety*** is to be wholeheartedly encouraged and restored! As seen earlier with the elements of the Prokeimenon,[48] the clue that this was the ancient practice of the Church is the fact that, in many instances, the "Alleluia" Verses are taken from the first verses of the particular Psalm of the day. For example, at the

---

[47] Ibid, p. 74.
[48] Cf. above, pp. 40-42.

Resurrectional Divine Liturgy for the week of tone 3, the verses are taken from **the first verses** of Psalm 30: "In You, O Lord, have I hoped! Let me never be put to shame!" (Psalm 30:1), and "Be a God of protection for me, a House of refuge, in order to save me!" (Psalm 30:2). Celebrating the entire Psalm, again at a brisk pace in order not to weigh down the rhythm of the service, will manifest to all present the centrality of the Gospel reading in the Divine Liturgy.

K. THE GOSPEL

Although the final decision regarding how the particulars of a liturgical service are done is in the hands of the diocesan bishop and the parish priest, if the choir director has a good and openly-communicative relationship with the pastor, he or she should try to encourage the priest to restore the chanting of the Prayer Before the Gospel in the Divine Liturgy. This, along with the "Alleluia" Verses, is an essential liturgical element that helps prepare the faithful for hearing the Gospel reading.[49] Also, if

---

[49] *Eucharist*, p. 76.

there is a deacon who will be reading the Gospel, a prayer of admonition by the priest or bishop is read, encouraging the deacon to "proclaim the Glad Tidings **with great power**, to the fulfillment of the Gospel...!". Therefore, the singing of the responses for the Gospel reading ("Amen."; a triple "Lord, have mercy."; "Glory to You, O Lord, glory to You!") should *also* be done **with great power**, to manifest the victorious message of the Good News!

L. THE CHERUBIKON

The Cherubic Hymn, or, more accurately, the Cherubikon, is the beginning of the offertory section of the Divine Liturgy that culminates in the Anaphora.[50] While it obviously functions to accompany the procession of the Holy Gifts during the Eucharistic (Great) Entrance, it is also an introduction to the whole eucharistic action from the Anaphora to Holy Communion, instructing the faithful that they must "lay aside all earthly cares" to prepare to receive Christ in Communion.[51]

---

[50] Taft, *Beyond East and West*, pp. 221-223.
[51] Ibid, p. 222.

The reason it is more correct to refer to this hymn as the "Cherubikon" is that, in the early Church, the singing of free-standing liturgical songs, that is, non-scriptural compositions, were a rarity, and this hymn was most likely a Psalm antiphon.[52] This shows that the Divine Liturgy had an introit antiphon at **both** entrances, the Gospel (Little) Entrance and the Eucharistic (Great) Entrance.[53] This manifests the "two-course" aspect of the Eucharistic Banquet, that of partaking of the readings from Scripture and of Holy Communion.[54]

What is significant for liturgical musicians today is that the Cherubikon was originally added to the Liturgy or replaced an earlier antiphonal Psalm at the Eucharistic (Great) Entrance, Psalm 23.[55] A restoration to celebrating the Cherubikon in this format would be preferable for a few reasons. The first is, it would clearly manifest the parallel of the

---

[52] Ibid, p. 221.
[53] Ibid.
[54] For a fuller discussion of the Cherubikon and its place in the Divine Liturgy, cf. Taft, Robert F., SJ, *The Great Entrance: The History of the Transfer of Gifts and other Preanaphoral Rites of the Liturgy of St John Chrysostom*, OCA 200, Rome, Italy, PIO, 1975 (hereafter referred to as "*Great Entrance*").
[55] Taft, *Beyond East and West*, p. 21. The Psalm references here are according to the Septuagint.

two Entrances of the Divine Liturgy. Second, it would eliminate the need, currently required with the **very** abridged modern version of the Cherubic Hymn, to repeat the words of the hymn in order to fill up time for the Entrance to take place. This is evident in **many** current settings of the hymn, where the people sing, "Let us, let us, let us, who mystically, mystically, mystically, represent the Cherubim, Cherubim, Cherubim", and so forth. This would be especially true at a Hierarchical Divine Liturgy, where the bishop, at the time of the Entrance, completes the commemorations at the Table of Oblation begun at the Proskomedia. This lengthens the time needed for the Entrance itself. Third and finally, this would restore the more ancient and authentic Orthodox liturgical practice of singing antiphons connected to the Psalter, and would invite **all** the people to participate by singing the refrain of the Cherubikon.

One way to do this would be for the people to sing the entire first half of what is now the Cherubic Hymn ("Let us, who mystically represent the Cherubim , and who sing the thrice-holy hymn to the life-creating Trinity, now lay aside all earthly cares!"). Then, a reader could chant, one at a time, the verses of Psalm 23. Then, **all** the people would respond with the refrain, "Let us lay aside all earthly cares!", interspersed between the Psalm verses chanted by the reader. Again, if the Entrance is taking longer for any reason (such as the aforementioned Hierarchical Divine Liturgy), the reader, after chanting the last verse of the Psalm, could go back and repeat the Psalm, starting with verse 1. After the commemorations are done and the Entrance itself is completed, the people would, as in the modern practice, sing the second half of what is now the Cherubic Hymn ("Amen. That we may receive the King of all, Who comes invisibly upborne by the angelic hosts! Alleluia! Alleluia! Alleluia!"). This is clearly an **essential** restoration that is actually being done, successfully and easily, in some parishes today.

M. THE ANAPHORA

We now come to **_the central_** section of the Divine Liturgy, the Anaphora, which means "lifting up," since the Holy Gifts of bread and wine are lifted up as an offering to God the Father, to become the Body and Blood of Christ through the descent of the Holy Spirit! However, this "chief section" of the Divine Liturgy is revealed as such, not in an autonomous isolation by itself, but only in relation to all other "parts" of the Liturgy that precede and follow it.[56] As such, being not only the central part of the service, but **a _corporate_ act** (the Eucharistic prayers of both St John Chrysostom and St Basil the Great are in the plural, saying "we" and "us", meaning **both** clergy **_and_** laity), **the Eucharistic prayers _must_ be said aloud for _all_ to hear and offer, in (again) this corporate worship!** The word "**_liturgy_**" means "**_common_** work" or "**_common_** action," and, as such, precludes the involvement of **_all_** the people of God, "[the] royal priesthood, [the] holy nation" (1 Peter 2:9).

For the liturgical musician, then, it is imperative that all arrangements and musical settings of the Anaphora that incorporate long, melismatic singing that "covers over" the Eucharistic Kanon be avoided and eliminated. One such setting is the "Theophanskaya" arrangement of the Anaphora. Being the essential and central part of the Divine Liturgy, with its victorious affirmation of the Holy Trinity and its emphasis on joy, praise, and thanksgiving, **_all_** settings of the Anaphora should be festive, celebratory, upbeat, joyous, and **_paschal!_** These settings should manifest the **_dialogical_** aspect

---

[56] Ibid, pp. 159-166, especially pp. 163-164.

of the Anaphora, of statement and response on the part of the main celebrant and the people!

This corporate aspect should reflect the complete setting of the Anaphora, through its conclusion. Therefore, the setting of the section beginning, "We praise You! We worship You!" should also **not** be long or melismatic, nor repeat the text of the hymn ("And we give thanks to You, O our God, O our God, O our God!") so as to cover over the Prayer of the Third Hour! For, again, this prayer as chanted by the main celebrant is in the **plural**: "O Lord, Who sent down Your most Holy Spirit upon Your Apostles at the third hour: Now, take not this same Holy Spirit from **us**, O Good One, but renew Him in **us** who pray to You!" Again, the **entire** Anaphora, from beginning to end, **must** be done **aloud corporately**, for it is the eucharistic assembly, **all together**, who offers the Divine Liturgy!

N.   THE LORD'S PRAYER

As our final liturgical element of preparation for the Holy Eucharist, we pray the Prayer of the Lord, Jesus Christ, Himself: "Our Father!" Here, we come to the apex of the acknowledgement of the

Ultimate Reality: that God is essentially, in His innermost being, Father! This was manifested earlier in the Anaphora, which is addressed, **not** to the Holy Trinity, but **exclusively** to God the Father: "For, You are God: ineffable, inconceivable, invisible, incomprehensible, ever-existing and eternally the same: You **and** Your only-begotten Son **and** Your Holy Spirit!" It is God the Father Who is the Origin and the Source of everyone and everything, **including** the other two Persons of the Holy Trinity, Who are properly called "the Son **of God**" and "the Spirit **of God**"! With this acknowledgement of what St Paul called our "adoption as sons" (Gal 4:5, from the Epistle reading for the Divine Liturgy of Christmas), we have completed the task of preparation. It is essential, therefore, that the singing of the Lord's Prayer be done joyously, festively, and in an assertive manner!

O.   THE KOINONIKON

As with the Gospel Entrance and the Eucharistic Entrance, the singing at the time of the receiving of Holy Communion, **for both clergy _and_ laity alike**, was in the form of a responsorial Psalm.[57] The current practice, of later development, consists of the following elements:

1) **Deacon:** "Let us be attentive!"
2) **Priest:** "Holy Things for the holy!"
3) **People:** "One is holy!"
4) Koinonikon: variable Psalm verse with triple "Alleluia!"
5) Manual acts (fraction, etc.)
6) Communion, with accompanying formulae.
7) **Priest:** "O God, save Your people and bless Your inheritance!"
8) **People:** "We have seen the true Light!"
9) **Priest:** [silently] "Blest is our God," [aloud] "always, now and ever and unto ages of ages!"
10) **People:** "Amen. Let our mouths be filled with Your praise, O Lord!" (Holy Gifts transferred from altar to table of oblation)

---

[57] Taft, *Beyond East and West*, pp. 227-230.

11) Litany and Prayer of Thanksgiving after Holy Communion.[58]

What was essential in the original liturgical practice was item 4, the Koinonikon, which was once a complete Psalm.[59] Item 10, "Let our mouths be filled," was added as a concluding refrain after the doxology of the Psalm.[60]

How can we restore some semblance of the original liturgical practice amidst this fractured block of elements? The first and obvious way is to stop treating the Communion of the clergy and the Communion of the people as totally different, unrelated liturgical acts, calling for the singing of so-called "concert pieces" during the former and the singing of a non-scriptural refrain ("Receive the Body of Christ!"), repeated *ad nauseum*, during the latter. Rather, for the time of Communion for *both* clergy *and* people, a responsorial Psalm should be sung throughout! This fits into the practice of the early

---

[58] Ibid, p. 227.
[59] Ibid, p. 228.
[60] Ibid.

Church for singing responsorial Psalmody at the time of processions, movement, and action. Then, once **everyone** who is going to receive the Eucharist does so and the celebrant says, "Lo! This has touched your lips, taken away your iniquities, and healed your sins!", **then** the people would sing the final triple "Alleluia!".

P. "HAVING BEHELD THE RESURRECTION OF CHRIST"

At this point, the service books call for the deacon in the sanctuary, during the time that the clergy are getting the Holy Gifts ready to be transferred back to the Table of Oblation, to chant a prayer. This "prayer," however, is actually a **hymn** that is sung as Post-Gospel Stikhera at Resurrectional Matins (beginning with, "Having beheld the Resurrection of Christ"). Therefore, in *some* parishes, the practice is for the people to sing these stikhera in the prescribed tone 6. This gives the clergy time to prepare the Holy Gifts to be transferred to the Table of Oblation. And, from the observation of the practice at Resurrectional Matins, this would return this liturgical element back to where it belongs, in its singing on the part of the people of God.

Q. LITURGY ENDING

What are now the concluding troparia of the koinonikon ("We have seen the true Light!" and "Let our mouths be filled") could then be celebrated as is currently done in parishes (one logical suggestion is to have the celebrant exclaim the ***entire*** doxology, "Blest is our God, always now and ever and unto ages of ages!", ***aloud!***). This liturgical "unit" or "block of elements" would then conclude with the Litany of Thanksgiving and its accompanying prayer and doxology, and the Prayer Before the Ambo.

6

SACRAMENTAL SERVICES

In the early Church, *all* sacraments were celebrated within the context of the Divine Liturgy. That is because the Eucharist, being the Sacrament of sacraments and manifesting the Kingdom of God, "colors" the perspective of all other sacraments and refers them to that very Kingdom.[61] Through the influence of the post-patristic "westernizing" theology that crept into the Orthodox Church, the sacraments lost their **corporate** status and became "individual" means of bestowing "grace".[62] This is what led to them being divorced from the celebration of the Eucharist to become independent services in their own right. However, as we now recover our true liturgical theology and **liturgical experience**, it is fitting, right, and imperative that we reunite the celebration of these sacraments within the context of the Divine Liturgy.

---

[61] Schmemann, *Liturgy and Tradition*, pp. 80-81.
[62] Ibid, pp. 72-74.

A. HOLY BAPTISM

In some dioceses and parishes, the restoration of the Sacrament of Holy Baptism with the Divine Liturgy is taking place (although this is **not d**one in the Greek practice). While the order and specifics for such a service need to be according to the instructions of the local bishop, the following seems to be the widely practiced order for such a service.[63]

The first part of the baptismal rite is known in the service books as the "Prayers at the Reception of the Catechumens." This section includes the Exorcisms, the Renunciation of Satan, the Conversion to Christ, and the Confession of Faith (the Creed). This section is celebrated in the narthex at the back of the church, and is done **_before_** the Divine Liturgy proper (with the doxology, "Blessed is the Kingdom!") begins. During all of these liturgical

---

[63] Cf. Schmemann, Alexander, *Of Water and the Spirit: A Liturgical Study of Baptism*, SVS Press, Crestwood, NY, 1974, pp. 115-121, and especially pp. 169-170. For Holy Baptism and Holy Chrismation served separately from the Divine Liturgy, cf. below, chapter 4, "Sacramental Services," pp. 251-265.

elements, the various prayers and exclamations are responded to with the appropriate singing of "Lord, have mercy." and "Amen." where called for.

When this initial section has been completed, the clergy, servers, initiate(s)-to-be-baptized, his or her sponsors (godparents), and his or her family members proceed from the narthex into the middle of the nave of the church. At this point, the Divine Liturgy proper begins, starting with the doxology, "Blessed is the Kingdom!" The people sing "Amen." in response, and this is followed by the Great Litany, with petitions appropriate to Baptism being added in. In this Baptismal Divine Liturgy, the singing of all three Antiphons and "Only-Begotten Son" is **omitted!**

After the Great Litany, the baptismal rites are celebrated: the Blessing of Water, the Anointing of Water, and the Anointing of the Initiate (both anointings done with "the oil of gladness"). Again, during all of these liturgical elements, the various prayers and exclamations are responded to with the appropriate singing of "Lord, have mercy.", "To You, O Lord.", and "Amen." where called for.

The Baptism proper (the triple immersion in water) now takes place. The people respond with an "Amen." at the ***three*** distinct sections of the baptismal exclamation: "The servant of God, [name], is Baptized, in the Name of the Father," ("Amen!"), "and of the Son," ("Amen!"), and of the Holy Spirit!" ("Amen!"). The reader ***then immediately*** chants Psalm 31 ("Blessed is he whose transgression is forgiven, whose sin is covered!").

Following this, the white baptismal garment is placed on the newly-baptized, as the celebrant chants, "The servant of God, [name], is clothed with the robe of gladness, in the Name of the Father, and of the Son, and of the Holy Spirit!" The people respond with "Amen!", and ***then immediately*** sing the following hymn, in tone 8:

> Grant unto me the robe of light, O most merciful Christ our God, Who clothe Yourself with light as with a garment!

After this, the Sacrament of Holy Chrismation is celebrated. This begins with a Prayer of Chrismation, the exclamation to which the people sing, "Amen." The newly-baptized is then anointed with the Holy Chrism. Similar to the anointing with the oil of gladness, the person is anointed over their entire body. At *each* point of anointing, the celebrant intones, "The seal of the gift of the Holy Spirit!", to which the people respond, *each* time, with "Amen." A final prayer is said, to which the people, again, respond by singing "Amen."

At this point, the Gospel Entrance is made, with the people singing, "Come, Let us Worship!" This is followed by the troparia and kontakia for the day.

Following these hymns, a special version of the Trisagion is sung. In place of "Holy God!", the people sing "As Many As Have Been Baptized!" The text is as follows: "As many as have been Baptized into Christ have put on Christ! Alleluia!" This is sung **three** times. At **each** of the **three** times, the celebrant leads the newly-chrismated, with his or her sponsors and his or her family members, around the baptismal font and the center icon analoi. After the third encircling and singing, the people continue by singing a full "Glory,... now and ever...!" During the singing of the "Glory!", the celebrant enters the sanctuary and the reader, carrying the Epistle book or Holy Bible, goes to receive a blessing. The newly-chrismated, along with his or her sponsors and his or her family members, then advance forward and stand at the foot of the ambo for the next part of the Divine Liturgy, until the faithful receive the Eucharist. The people then sing an abbreviation of the hymn ("Have put on Christ! Alleluia!"), followed by a final full "As Many As Have Been Baptized!"

At this point, the reader is at his or her place in the center of the church. **Two** prokeimena are sung here: the one for the day, and the following Prokeimenon for Baptism, in tone 3:[64]

> The Lord is my Light and my Salvation!
> Whom should I fear?

---

[64] For the format of chanting *two* prokeimena, see above, pp. 207-208.

Two Epistle readings are then chanted: the one for the day, and the one for the Sacrament of Baptism (Romans 6:3-11). This is followed by the ***usual two*** "Alleluia!" verses, since there are ***no*** special "Alleluia!" verses called for in the Sacrament of Baptism.

Then, *two* Gospel readings are chanted: one for the day, and one for the Sacrament of Baptism (Matthew 28:16-20). Since the person proclaiming the two Gospel readings only pauses slightly (with ***no*** special announcement) between the first and second readings, this does not affect the choir director and Church singers. The responses sung are done as prescribed at a regular Divine Liturgy.

At the time when the faithful receive the Eucharist, the newly-baptized, his or her sponsors, and his or her family members all receive the Eucharist first, followed by the rest of the faithful. Before this, however, the churching of the newly-baptized takes place, with the celebrant bringing the person from the back to the front of the church, pausing as various places with exclamations ("The servant of God, [name], is churched...!", "In the midst of the congregation, [he, she] will sing praises to You!"), to which there are **no sung responses**. **After** the churching, however, the people sing the Prayer of St Symeon ("Lord, Now Let Your Servant Depart in Peace!") in tone 6.

The Divine Liturgy continues. At the point where the singing of "Blessed Be the Name of the Lord!" is called for, it is appropriate to sing this hymn **only twice**. The tonsuring of the newly-baptized then takes place, with the appropriate responses ("Lord, have mercy.", "Amen.") at the usual places.

This is followed by the Washing Off of the Holy Chrism and the Tonsuring. Again, during these sections, the various prayers and exclamations are responded to with the appropriate singing of "Lord, have mercy.", "To You, O Lord.", and "Amen." where called for. All of this is **immediately** followed by the **third** and **final** singing of "Blessed Be the Name of the Lord!" The rest of the Divine Liturgy concludes in the usual order.

B. HOLY MATRIMONY

In some dioceses and parishes, the restoration of the Sacrament of Matrimony with the Divine Liturgy is taking place (although this is **not** done in the Greek practice). While the order and specifics for such a service need to be according to the instructions of the local bishop, the following seems to be the widely-practiced order for such a service.[65]

The betrothal takes place at the entrance from the narthex into the nave of the church. For this part of the service, for those who are singing, the people respond with "Lord, have mercy." and "Amen." where it is appropriate. This betrothal **may** take place the evening before, at the end of Vespers.[66]

The priest (or bishop) leads the couple to the center of the church for the crowning. The celebrant intones, "Glory to You, our God, glory to You!" The

---

[65] Cf. Meyendorff, John, *Marriage: An Orthodox Perspective*, SVS Press, Crestwood, NY, 1984, Chapter VIII, "A Liturgical Suggestion," pp. 42-43. For Holy Matrimony served separately from the Divine Liturgy, cf. below, chapter 4, "Sacramental Services," pp. 267-285.

[66] Meyendorff, *Marriage*, p. 43.

people then sing "Glory to You, our God, glory to You!" The celebrant then intones a set of verses. **After _each_ verse**, the people respond by singing "Glory to You, our God, glory to You!"

At _this_ point, the Divine Liturgy begins with the doxology, "Blessed is the Kingdom!" The Great Litany is then celebrated, with its appropriately sung responses. In this Matrimonial Divine Liturgy, the singing of all three Antiphons and "Only-Begotten Son" is **omitted!** After the Great Litany, the three wedding prayers are said, with the appropriate singing of "Lord, have mercy." and "Amen."

Then, the crowning takes place. The celebrant crowns each person of the wedding couple, "In the Name of the Father, and of the Son, and of the Holy Spirit." In both cases, the people respond by singing, "Amen."

After this, the Gospel Entrance is made, with the singing of "Come, Let Us Worship!" The troparia and kontakia for the day are then sung, followed by the singing of the Trisagion. Then, **two** prokeimena are then chanted: the one for the day, followed by the following Prokeimenon for Matrimony, in tone 8:[67]

> You have set upon their heads crowns of precious stones! They asked life of You, and You gave it to them!

Two Epistle readings are chanted: the one for the day, and the one for the Sacrament of Matrimony (Ephesians 5:20-33). This is followed by the ***usual two*** "Alleluia!" verses, since there are *no* special "Alleluia!" verses called for in the Sacrament of Matrimony.

Then, ***two*** Gospel readings are chanted: one for the day, and one for the Sacrament of Matrimony (John 2:1-12). Since the person proclaiming the two Gospel readings only pauses slightly (with ***no*** special announcement) between the first and second readings, this does not affect the choir director and Church singers. The responses

---

[67] For the format of chanting *two* prokeimena, see above, pp. 207-208.

sung are done as prescribed at a regular Divine Liturgy.

The rest of the service continues to be celebrated. After the laity have received the Eucharist, the bridal couple *may* partake of a "common cup" (as is done when the Sacrament of Matrimony is separated from the Divine Liturgy), with the usual responses of "Lord, have mercy." and "Amen." being sung.[68]

The Divine Liturgy continues. At the point where the singing of "Blessed Be the Name of the Lord!" is called for, it is appropriate to sing this hymn *only* **twice**. A triple procession then occurs, with the main celebrant leading the bridal couple three times around the analoi holding the icon in the middle of the church. During the *first* encircling, the people sing, "Rejoice, O Isaiah! A Virgin is with Child, and will bear a Son, Emmanuel, both God and Man! And 'Orient' is His Name, Whom, magnifying, we called the Virgin 'Blessed!'" During the *second* encircling, the people sing, "O holy martyrs, who fought the good fight and have received your crowns, entreat the Lord that He may have mercy upon us!" During

---

[68] Meyendorff, *Marriage*, p. 43.

the ***third*** encircling, the people sing, "Glory to You, O Christ God, the Apostles' Boast, the martyrs' Joy, whose preaching was the consubstantial Trinity!"

The removal of the crowns by the main celebrant then takes place, with the usual responses of "Lord, have mercy." and "Amen." being sung. This is ***immediately*** followed by the ***third*** and ***final*** singing of "Blessed Be the Name of the Lord!" The rest of the Divine Liturgy concludes in the usual order.

This Matrimonial Divine Liturgy would ***not***, of course, be celebrated in the cases of "mixed marriages" or "re-marriages." In those cases, the joint partaking of the Eucharist being excluded, the Sacrament of Matrimony would be celebrated separately from the Divine Liturgy.[69]

C. FUNERAL

In some dioceses and parishes, the restoration of the Funeral with the Divine Liturgy is taking place, especially if the newly-departed Orthodox Christian

---

[69] Ibid.

was a seriously active member of the Church (although this is *not* done in the Greek practice). While the order and specifics for such a service need to be according to the instructions of the local bishop, the following seems to be the widely-practiced order for such a service.[70]

This service is similar to a Vesperal Liturgy, where the first half of the service is a Great Vespers that then transitions into the second half of the Divine Liturgy. Here, the first half of the service is the Funeral service, which then "morphs" into the second half of the Divine Liturgy.

If the body of the newly-departed in his or her casket has not yet been brought into the church, the singers stand vigilantly on the sidewalk in the front of the church. When the hearse drives up and the body of the departed is wheeled into the church, the singers lead the procession, singing the *slow* Processional "Holy God!" ("Holy God! Holy Mighty! Holy Immortal! Have mercy on us!") ***repeatedly***

---

[70] For the Funeral served separately from the Divine Liturgy, cf. below, *Volume 2*, chapter 6, "Funeral, Interment, and Memorial."

until the casket of the departed is in the center of the church.

The service begins with the eucharistic doxology, "Blessed is the Kingdom!" The **people** respond by **singing**, "Amen.", then sing the Trisagion ("Holy God! Holy Mighty! Holy Immortal! Have mercy on us!") **three** times. A **reader** then reads the Trisagion Prayers ("O Most Holy Trinity, have mercy on us!"; a **triple** "Lord, have mercy."; and a full "Glory,... now and ever...!"), followed by the Lord's Prayer. After the exclamation, "For, Yours are the Kingdom, and the power, and the glory,...!", the reader chants, "Amen.", then "Come, let us worship God, our King! Come, let us worship and fall down before Christ, our King and our God! Come, let us worship and fall down before Christ Himself (or, "the very Christ"), our King and our God!", then chants Psalm 90 ("He who dwells in the shelter of the Most High...!"), followed by a full "Glory,... now and ever...!", and then, **three** times, "Alleluia! Alleluia! Alleluia! Glory to You, O God!"

The celebrant then chants the verses of the First Stasis from Psalm 118. In between each verse, the people respond with *one* "Alleluia!" The celebrant then chants a full "Glory,... now and ever...!", and the people respond one more time with a single "Alleluia!"

The celebrant then chants the verses of the Second Stasis from Psalm 118. In between each verse, the people respond with, "Have mercy upon Your servant!" The celebrant then chants a full "Glory,... now and ever...!", and the people respond one more time with, "Have mercy upon Your servant!"

The celebrant then chants the verses of the Third Stasis from Psalm 118. In between each verse, the people respond with **one** "Alleluia!" The celebrant then chants a full "Glory,... now and ever...!", and the people respond one more time with a single "Alleluia!"

The people then sing, "Blessed are You, O Lord! Teach me Your statutes!" (which is the refrain of this hymn) in tone 5, with its interspersed verses. This hymn ends with the triple singing of, "Alleluia! Alleluia! Alleluia! Glory to You, O God!"

There then follows a Little Litany: two petitions calling for "Lord, have mercy." as the response; one petition calling for "Grant it, O Lord." as the response; one more petition calling for "Lord, have mercy." as the response; and an exclamation, to which the people respond by singing, "Amen." (This is the standard format for *all* Little Litanies at a Funeral, Funeral Divine Liturgy, and Memorial service.)

Then, the people sing Kathisma Hymns in tone 5, the first one beginning, "Give rest with the just, O our Savior, unto Your servants."

This is followed by the Funeral Kanon, in tone 6. Here, in popular practice, **only** odes 1, 3, 6, and 9 are celebrated. Ode 1 begins, "When Israel passed on foot over the sea,…." Ode 3 starts, "There is none so holy as You, O Lord my God,…." Ode 6 leads off with, "When Israel passed on foot over the sea,…." Ode 9 begins, "It is not possible for men to see God,…." After **each** and **every** ode, the celebrant intones, "Give rest, O Lord, to the soul of Your servant who has fallen asleep!" The people then sing this very same, "Give rest, O Lord,…!" The celebrant then chants, for odes 1, 3, and 6, "Glory to the Father, and to the Son, and to the Holy Spirit!" For ode 9, the celebrant chants, "Let us bless the

Father, and the Son, and the Holy Spirit, the Lord!" In **all** of these instances, the people respond by singing, "Now and ever and unto ages of ages! Amen."

In some parishes, there is an effort to restore the troparia of the Kanon chanted by a reader. In that case, the ode is sung, the reader chants the troparia, and **then** the celebrant begins intoning, "Give rest, O Lord,...!"

After ode 6, the Kontakion ("With the saints, give rest,...."), in tone 6, and the Oikos ("You, only, are Immortal,..."), in tone 8. These are then followed by **either** the chanting of "Give rest, O Lord,...!" **or** by the chanted troparia and **then**, "Give rest, O Lord,...!"

After the Kanon, the Beatitudes are celebrated. The main celebrant intones the first four verses of the Beatitudes, then the people respond by singing, "Remember us, O Lord, when You come in Your Kingdom!", and after each set of verses. The celebrant then chants "Glory to the Father, and to the Son, and to the Holy Spirit.", followed by a verse. The people again sing, "Remember us, O Lord, when You come in Your Kingdom!" The celebrant chants,

"Now and ever and unto ages of ages. Amen.", followed by a verse. The people sing "Remember us, O Lord, when You come in Your Kingdom!" a final time.

At this point, the service transitions into the Divine Liturgy through the celebration of the Prokeimenon. For the Funeral, this is in tone 6, and states, "Blessed is the way in which you shall walk today, O soul! For, a place of rest is prepared for you!" The reader chants this, then the people sing it. The reader then chants a response verse ("To You, O Lord, will I call! O my God, be not silent to me!"), and the people sing the Prokeimenon verse ("Blessed is the way…!") again. The reader then chants the first half of the Prokeimenon verse ("Blessed is the way in which you shall walk today, O soul!"), after which the people sing the second half of the verse ("For, a place of rest is prepared for you!").

The reader then chants the Funeral Epistle (1 Thessalonians 4:13-17). This is followed by the "Alleluia!" verses: the reader chants, "And with your spirit! Alleluia! Alleluia! Alleluia!" The people sing a triple "Alleluia!" The reader chants the first verse,

"Blessed are they whom You have chosen and taken, O Lord!" The people sing a triple "Alleluia!" The reader chants the second verse, "Their memory is from generation to generation!" The people sing a final triple "Alleluia!"

The Gospel is then proclaimed (John 5:24-30). This is followed by the sermon, and the rest of the Divine Liturgy.

After the triple singing of "Blessed Be the Name of the Lord!", the people sing the Troparia for the Departed, in tone 4, beginning, "With the souls of the righteous departed,...."

This is followed by an Augmented Litany. Just like at Daily Vespers, the Augmented Litany here begins with the petition, "Have mercy on us, O God,....", and the people responding with a **triple** "Lord, have mercy." ***right from this first petition***. There are three petitions that call for this triple "Lord, have mercy." as the response. Then comes a petition whereby the people respond with, "Grant it, O Lord." Then, another petition that calls for, as a response, a **single** "Lord, have mercy." This is followed by a long prayer and an exclamation, to which the people respond by singing, "Amen."

After this, the celebrant reads the Final Prayer of Absolution over the body of the departed. The usual sung responses of "Lord, have mercy." and "Amen." occur where appropriate.

The Dismissal then follows, with its exclamations and sung responses: "Wisdom! Most Holy Theotokos, save us!" ("More honorable than the Cherubim,....."), and "Glory to You, O Christ, our God and our Hope, glory to You!" (a full "Glory,... now and ever...!", a triple "Lord, have mercy.", and "Father [or, "Master"; or, "Most Blessed Master"], bless!"). The dismissal prayer is intoned, concluding with an exclamation, to which the people *usually* respond with a double "Amen." (or, it *could* be a single "Amen.")

The celebrant then takes the censer and, standing on the solea and facing the Altar, intones "Memory Eternal!" for the newly-departed person. The people then sing, "Memory Eternal!" *three* times, followed by "[His, Her] soul will dwell with the blessed!"

As the people come forward to pay their respects to the departed person, recessional hymns are sung. These usually consist of "Come, Let Us

Give the Last Kiss" (in tone 2) and "The Lord is My Shepherd" (in tone 8). If it is during the Pascha season, "Let God Arise!" may also be added here.

As the pallbearers wheel the body of the deceased back out to the hearse, the singers again lead the procession, singing the *slow* Processional "Holy God!" ("Holy God! Holy Mighty! Holy Immortal! Have mercy on us!") **repeatedly** until the casket is placed in the hearse.

7
THE FESTAL CYCLE

A. VESPERAL LITURGY

Today, in our hectic urban society, where most parishioners have to work during the weekdays of Monday through Friday, **many** parishes are celebrating feast days during the week with a Vesperal Divine Liturgy (although this is **not** done in the Greek practice). Basically, the first half of the service is the Great Vespers portion, which then smoothly transitions into the Divine Liturgy part of the service. Its standard outline is as follows.

The celebrant intones, just as at a regular Divine Liturgy, the doxology, "Blessed is the Kingdom of the Father, and of the Son, and of the Holy Spirit, now and ever and unto ages of ages!" The people respond by singing, "Amen.", and then **immediately** singing, "Come, Let Us Worship!" and Psalm 103 ("Bless the Lord, O My Soul!").

Because Kathisma 1 from the Psalter (Psalms 1-3), beginning with "Blessed is the Man," is prescribed **only** for Saturday evening Resurrectional Vespers, when there is a Great Vespers for any other evening of the week (Sunday through Friday evenings), "Blessed is the Man" is **not** sung (although "Blessed is the Man" is sometimes prescribed [not always] for the Vespers of feast days that occur on other weekdays)! If the prescribed Kathisma for the Great Vespers for the particular evening of the week is available (as is the case in most monasteries), that may be sung at this point. Otherwise, the people go directly from the Great Litany to the singing of "Lord, I Call Upon You."

After the singing of "Lord, I Call Upon You" and "Let My Prayer Arise," there is a refrain verse by a reader, and then there are festal *stikhera* (sets of sung verses), with refrain verses in between that are chanted by the reader. Then, the reader chants the "Glory...now and ever..." and the people sing the stikheron relating to the feast and Christ. There may be up to ten stikhera sung before the "Glory."

During the singing of the "Glory..., now and ever..." stikheron, the clergy and servers process from the sanctuary out into the nave, for the Vesperal Entrance. The priest or deacon then raises the censer and says, "Wisdom! Let us be attentive!" The people then sing the Vesperal Entrance hymn,

"Gladsome Light," which is the central hymn of Vespers, acknowledging Christ as the Light of the world! The clergy and servers then process back into the sanctuary.

The clergy go to the high place at the back of the altar, and then the Evening Prokeimenon is chanted. (In the Byzantine tradition, this Evening Prokeimenon is usually omitted, and there is also a great variety of practices in that tradition on how this liturgical element is celebrated. As always, the local custom should be observed.) The clergy begin by chanting, "Wisdom! Let us be attentive! Peace be with you all!," and then continue, "The Prokeimenon is in the [1st through 8th] tone." The main verse of the Prokeimenon is then chanted. The people respond by singing the main verse of the Prokeimenon in the prescribed tone. This is sung by the people after each verse is chanted by the clergy. After the last verse is chanted, the priest or deacon then chants the first half of the verse. The people then respond with the second half of the verse to conclude the Prokeimenon.

After the Evening Prokeimenon, three Old (or, sometimes, New) Testament readings are read at this point. If so, there will usually be three readings, though there can be more.

Then, there is a Little Litany celebrated, followed by the singing of the troparion and Kontakion of the feast, as is done at a regular Divine Liturgy. At this point, the Trisagion is celebrated, and the rest of the Divine Liturgy follows, as usual.

B. VIGILS OF THE NATIVITY OF CHRIST AND OF THEOPHANY

The Vigil service for the feasts of both the Nativity of Christ (Christmas) and Theophany are comprised of Grand (Great) Compline and Festal Matins. This is because Great Vespers for both feasts had already been celebrated earlier in the Vesperal Liturgy of St Basil the Great. Celebrating the Vigil, as prescribed in the Typikon, in parishes can be quite lengthy and heavy. Therefore, many parishes abbreviate the service to some extent. Since the Festal Matins is the more central service for the feasts and contains more of the festal elements for each feast, it is more appropriate to abbreviate the liturgical elements of Grand Compline. The following is an outline of Grand

Compline for these two feasts that both retains the key liturgical elements of the service and keeps the Vigil service to a managable length.

    After the initial exclamation ("Blessed is our God, always now and ever and unto ages of ages!") and the responsorial "Amen," a reader chants "Glory to You, our God, glory to You!", "O Heavenly King!", the Trisagion Prayers, and the Lord's Prayer. Following the exclamation ("For, Yours are the Kingdom and the power and the glory...!") and the "Amen," the reader continues with "Lord, have mercy" twelve times, a full "Glory,...now and ever...!", "Come, let us worship God our King!", and three Psalms: Psalm 4 (beginning, "Answer me when I call, O God of my right!"), Psalm 6 (beginning, "O Lord, rebuke me not in Your anger, nor chasten me in Your wrath!"), and Psalm 12 (beginning, "Help, Lord! For, there are no longer any who are godly!").[71] The reader then chants a full "Glory,... now and ever...!", then "Alleluia! Alleluia! Alleluia! Glory to You, O God!" three times, a triple "Lord, have mercy.", and another full "Glory,... now and

---

[71] Again, the numbering of the Psalms is according to the Septuagint.

ever...!" The reader (or, another reader, perhaps) then chants another three Psalms: Psalm 24 (beginning, "To You, O Lord, I lift up my soul! O my God, in You I trust!"), Psalm 30 (beginning, "I will extol You, O Lord, for You have drawn me up!"), and Psalm 90 (beginning, "He who dwells in the shelter of the Most High!"). Again, the reader then chants a full "Glory,... now and ever...!", then "Alleluia! Alleluia! Alleluia! Glory to You, O God!" **three** times, a *triple* "Lord, have mercy.", and another full "Glory,... now and ever...!" As mentioned in previous chapters, the centrality of the Psalter in our liturgical services goes back to the time of the very early Church, and should *not* be compromised in favor of other liturgical elements.

Following this, "God is With Us!" is celebrated. This *is* a key liturgical element of Grand Compline. The deacon chants the full exclamation: "God is with us! Understand, all you nations, and submit yourselves! For, God is with us!" The people then sing this entire exclamation, in tone 4, in full voice. The deacon then chants the prayer that begins, "Hear this, all you ends of the Earth! Submit yourselves, you mighty ones! Even if your strength returns, you will be overthrown once more!..." The

The Festal Cycle

people then repeatedly sing an abbreviated ending of the exclamation: "For, God is with us!" In *some* parishes, this is done *very* quietly during the entire chanting of the prayer by the deacon, which, in effect, ends up **covering over** the prayer itself. For this reason, in **other** parishes, after the deacon chants each paragraph of the prayer, the people then sing the abbreviated ending, with the deacon **waiting** until the singing is concluded before going on with the prayer. That way, everyone in church gets to hear and meditate on the entire prayer. Obviously, this second method of celebrating the prayer is the **preferred** one. After completing the prayer with a full "Glory,… now and ever…!", the deacon full proclaims the entire exclamation again: "God is with us! Understand, all you nations, and submit yourselves! For, God is with us!" The people then sing this entire exclamation fully, one last time.

After this, the reader chants some prayers: "The day is past! I thank You, O Lord! Grant me to pass this evening and this night without sin, and save me, O my Savior! Glory to the Father, and to the Son, and to the Holy Spirit! The day is past! I glorify You, O Master! Grant me to pass this evening and this night without giving offense, and save me, O my

Savior! Now and ever and unto ages of ages! Amen. The day is past! I sing to You, O Holy One! Grant me to pass this evening and this night free from temptation, and save me, O my Savior!"

Following this, the service calls for the main celebrant to chant various verses of supplication (beginning with "All-holy sovereign Lady Theotokos, pray for us sinners!"), which are then repeated by the people singing them. These verses of supplication **can** appropriately be **omitted** from the service without removing a key liturgical element.

At this point, the service usually then proceeds to a reader chanting the Trisagion Prayers and the Lord's Prayer. **However**, since the service **also** calls for these prayers to be done **again** following Psalms 50, 101, and the Prayer of Manasseh, where it more appropriately functions as a **concluding** element to that part of the service, the celebration of the Trisagion Prayers and the Lord's Prayer at **this** point in the service **can** and **should** be **omitted**.

After this, the troparion of the feast is sung: for Christmas, it is, "Your Nativity, O Christ our God,...!", in tone 4; for Theophany, it is, "When You, O Lord, were Baptized in the Jordan,...!", in tone 1.

The service then calls for the reader to chant "Lord, have mercy" forty times, followed by "More honorable than the Cherubim" and "In the Name of the Lord, Father bless!", with the celebrant responding with, "Through the prayers of our holy fathers,…!" This section of the service *can* appropriately be **omitted**.

After this, the troparion of the feast is sung: for Christmas, it is, "Your Nativity, O Christ our God,…!", in tone 4; for Theophany, it is, "When You, O Lord, were Baptized in the Jordan,…!", in tone 1.

The service then calls for the reader to chant "Lord, have mercy" forty times, followed by "More honorable than the Cherubim" and "In the Name of the Lord, Father bless!", with the celebrant responding with, "Through the prayers of our holy fathers,…!" This section of the service *can* appropriately be **omitted**.

Following this, the reader chants Psalms 69 and 142, and then the Great Doxology is celebrated. [**_Note:_** The service book calls for the Lesser Doxology, to be chanted by a reader (which is still celebrated that way in the Byzantine tradition).[72] However, most parishes have the people sing this as a Great Doxology.]

After the Great Doxology, Litya stikhera are sung, and the Litya petitions of a litany follow.

There now follows the Apostikha. For Christmas, the people sing, "A great and marvelous wonder!" in tone 2. The reader chants the verse, "The Lord said to my Lord, 'Sit at My right hand, until I make Your enemies Your footstool!'" The people then sing, "Today, the Virgin gives Birth to the Maker of all!" in tone 3. The reader chants the verse, "From the womb, before the morning star, have I begotten you!" The people sing, "When the Lord Jesus was Born!" in tone 3. The reader chants, "Glory,...Spirit!" The people sing, "Make glad, O Jerusalem!" in tone 4. The reader chants, "Now and ever...Amen." The people sing, "You have come to dwell in a cave!" in tone 4.

For Theophany, the people sing, "Seeing You, O Christ our God!" in tone 2. The reader chants the verse, "The sea saw it and fled! Jordan turned

---

[72] Mother Mary and Ware, Archimandrite Kallistos, *The Festal Menaion*, Faber and Faber, London, 1977 (hereafter referred to as "*Menaion*"), p. 262.

The Festal Cycle

back!'" The people then sing, "The waters saw You, O God!" in tone 2. The reader chants the verse, "What ails you, O sea, that you flee? O Jordan, that you turn back?" The people sing, "Today, the Maker of Heaven and Earth!" in tone 2. The reader chants a full "Glory,…now and ever…!" The people sing, "Seeing the Sun, Who came from a Virgin!" in tone 6.

The people then sing the troparion for the feast: for Christmas, it is, "Your Nativity, O Christ our God,….!", in tone 4; for Theophany, it is, "When You, O Lord, were Baptized in the Jordan,…!", in tone 1.

Although it is not called for in the service books, in **many** parishes the people sing, "Blessed be the Name of the Lord, henceforth and forevermore!" **three** times.

The celebrant comes out of the sanctuary, stands on the ambo, and blesses the people, as he intones, "The blessing of the Lord be upon you, through His grace and love for mankind, always now and ever and unto ages of ages!" The people sing, in response, "Amen."

The celebration of Matins then begins **immediately**, with the people singing, "Glory to God in the highest!" **three** times, and "O Lord, open my lips!" **two** times.

8
LENT, HOLY WEEK, AND PASCHA

A. FORGIVENESS VESPERS

The preparatory Sundays leading up to the beginning of Great Lent have a nominal amount of liturgical elements specific to the Sunday at hand. Most of them consist of a kontakion, along with the singing of "Open the Doors of Repentance" and "By the Waters of Babylon." Therefore, there are no liturgical elements that need to be discussed here.

Regarding Forgiveness Vespers, the service that inaugurates Great Lent itself, there are two points to make here. One does not concern liturgical music as such, and that is the fact that the service should be celebrated at a time in the specific parish when the maximum number of parishioners would be able to attend and participate in the service.

The other point *does* concern liturgical music. This is concerning the singing of the Paschal verses that begin with, "Let God Arise!" In some parishes, there is the erroneous practice of singing these verses and stopping right before the singing of the

Paschal troparion, "Christ is Risen from the dead, trampling down death by death, and, upon those in the tombs, bestowing life!" The mistaken thought process behind this practice says that, since it is the beginning of Great Lent and *not* yet the time of Pascha, it is inappropriate to sing this troparion.

What the proponents of this practice fail to realize is the point so eloquently articulated by Fr Alexander Schmemann. He said, "When a man leaves on a journey, he must know where he is going. Thus with Lent. Above all, Lent is a spiritual journey and its destination is Easter, 'the Feast of feasts.' It is the preparation for the 'fulfillment of Pascha, the true Revelation'."[73] Concerning Forgiveness Vespers itself, Fr Schmemann says, " At the end of the service all the faithful approach the priest and one another asking for mutual forgiveness. But as they perform this rite of reconciliation, as Lent is inaugurated by this movement of love, reunion, and brotherhood, the choir sings the Paschal hymns. We will have to wander forty days through the desert of Lent. Yet at the end shines already the light of Easter, the light of

---

[73] Schmemann, *Great Lent*, p. 11.

the Kingdom.[74] Therefore, to keep in mind during all of Great Lent what the *goal* of this journey is, the Paschal hymns, **concluding with the Paschal troparion**, are fully celebrated! The singing of these verses and troparion, then, should **not** eliminated or abbreviated whatsoever.

B. KANON OF ST. ANDREW OF CRETE

During the first week of Lent and on the Thursday of the fifth week, Grand Compline with the Kanon of St Andrew of Crete is celebrated. A few liturgical elements of that service need to be discussed here.

"God is With Us"

As mentioned in the previous chapter,[75] "God is With Us!" is done in *some* parishes *very* quietly during the entire chanting of the prayer by the

---

[74] Ibid, p. 30.
[75] Pp. 122-123.

deacon, which, in effect, ends up **covering over** the prayer itself. For this reason, in *other* parishes, after the deacon chants each paragraph of the prayer, the people then sing the abbreviated ending, with the deacon **waiting** until the singing is concluded before going on with the prayer. That way, everyone in church gets to hear and meditate on the entire prayer. Obviously, this second method of celebrating the prayer is the **preferred** one.

Verses of Supplication

The same point needs to be stressed when the Verses of Supplication are done. They start with the verse, "All-holy sovereign Lady Theotokos, pray for us sinners!" The way these verses are celebrated is when the main celebrant exits the sanctuary and stands on the solea before the Royal Doors, chanting a series of petitions. After *each* petition, the people sing this *same* petition. As was the case with "God is With Us!", these verses are done in **some** parishes *very* quietly during the entire chanting of the verses by the main celebrant, which, in effect, ends up **covering over** the verses themselves. Again, it is preferable for the main celebrant to **wait** until the singing of one verse is complete before chanting the next verse.

"Remain With Us, O Lord of Hosts!"

The singing of the refrain, "Remain with us, O Lord of hosts! In affliction, we have no other Helper but You! O Lord of hosts, have mercy on us!", interspersed with the verses of Psalms 148, 149, and 150, is a lengthy liturgical element. Because of that, the singers in many parishes sing this in such a rushed and frenzied manner that the words sound unintelligible. While it preferred to sing this at a light and moving pace rather than in a dragging and plodding manner, the singing of this should *not* be done in such a way that the meaning of the text is obscured.

C. THE LITURGY OF THE PRESANCTIFIED GIFTS

In essence, the Liturgy of the Presanctified Gifts is a service of Communion following Vespers.[76] Being a service where the Holy Gifts were sanctified at the previous Sunday Divine Liturgy (from where the service gets its name), it is basically a Vesperal Liturgy with*out* an Anaphora that contains the **penitential** elements of the services of Great Lent. Yet, being a service where Holy Communion is received, it retains a spark of that ***joyful***, celebratory character of a regular Divine Liturgy. The Liturgy of the Presanctified Gifts, then, is the perfect example of a Lenten service that manifests that unique characteristic of Great Lent that Fr Alexander Schmemann referred to as "***bright sadness.***"[77] It therefore behooves those whose ministry it is to sing the responses at the divine services to celebrate this service in a manner that keeps in mind these two seemingly contradictory yet complimentary perspectives, that of the penitential "***sadness***" of the

---

[76] Schmemann, *Great Lent*, p. 52.
[77] Ibid, pp. 31-33.

Lenten season and the joyful, Pascha-anticipatory "**brightness**" of the Divine Liturgy.

Doxology, Psalm 103, and the Great Litany

The eucharistic centrality of the service is manifested at the very beginning with the very same **eschatological** doxology taken from the regular Divine Liturgy itself: "Blest is the Kingdom of the Father, and of the Son, and of the Holy Spirit, now and ever and unto ages of ages!" Therefore, the responsatory "Amen" sung by the people should be sung in the same joyful, assertive manner as done at a regular Divine Liturgy.

This is followed by the chanting of Psalm 103 by a reader, as is done at a Daily Lenten Vespers. As can be seen by an examination of the rest of the service, the use of readings and stikhera from the Psalter constitute a **major** element of this service. Being one of the most ancient practices of Orthodox services, inherited from the practice in Old Testament Israel itself, this element should in no wise be abbreviated, abridged, or minimized.

Following Psalm 103, the Great Litany is then celebrated as it is at the beginning of all liturgical services. What has been said previously concerning the singing of the responses in a manner that allows the petitions to be fully heard and understood, applies here as well.

"Lord, I Call Upon You" and Stikhera

The service continues, following the usual ordo for Vespers, with the singing of "Lord, I Call Upon You" and the accompanying stikhera. The thematic content of these stikhera consist mostly on the penitential need for repentance and inner reflection that is so great a part of the Lenten effort. The manner and style of singing these stikhera, then, should be done that takes into consideration both the need for repentance with the hope of forgiveness and salvation from the all-merciful Lord.

"Gladsome Light"

As reflected upon in chapter 3 in the discussion of Vespers,[78] "Gladsome Light" is the central thematic liturgical element of Vespers, focusing on Christ as the Light of the world. That this element is even more central in the Liturgy of the Presanctified Gifts is shown after the singing of this hymn, when, after the Second Prokeimenon is chanted, the main celebrant emerges from the sanctuary to stand on the ambo facing the people (who are penitentially prostrated on the floor) and, holding both a candle (representing Christ) and the censer (representing the sanctification by the Holy Spirit) raises up both as he exclaims, "Wisdom! Let us be attentive! The light of Christ illumines all!" The fact that this rite takes place between the two Old Testament readings manifests the teaching of the Church that Christ is the fulfillment of the Old Testament prophecies and the journey of God's people.

---

[78] Cf. above, pp. 39-42.

Therefore, the singing of "Gladsome Light" should be done in the same solemn yet celebratory manner that is sung at a regular Vespers.

Prokeimena, "The Light of Christ", and Old Testament Readings

As mentioned above, the use of the Psalter is a major component of the Liturgy of the Presanctified Gifts. And, inasmuch as it is the function of the Prokeimena to prepare the people and introduce the Old Testament readings, the chanting of the verses of the **_full_** Psalm for each Prokeimenon should be restored. In fact, the inclusion of a full Psalm is a standard practice at Lenten services. For example, in many parishes, immediately after the singing of "Lord, I Call Upon You" and "Let My Prayer Arise," the reader at a regular Vespers will begin with the appropriate verse before the first stikheron ("Bring my soul out of prison," "Let Your ears be attentive," etc.). However, at **Lenten** Vespers, the reader begins with the verses of the **_full_** Psalm, "Set a guard over my mouth, O Lord!" This is further confirmed in the rubrics of the Lenten services, which call for the kathismata of the Psalter to be chanted **twice** throughout the week at the services of Vespers and Matins.[79] Therefore, the restoration of the ancient Church practice of celebrating the *entire* Psalm for the Prokeimenon at this Presanctified Liturgy, as with the services of regular Vespers and the regular Divine Liturgy, should be restored.

Following each Prokeimenon, an Old Testament reading is chanted, the first one from Genesis and the second one from Proverbs. In many parishes, two different readers are used, one for the First Prokeimenon and Genesis reading, and the other for the Second Prokeimenon and Proverbs reading. What was said in previous chapters of the importance of chanting the readings from Scripture in a clear, concise, prayerful, and understandable manner, cannot be overemphasized here. In most parishes, it is the choir director who is given the task of training parish readers and instructing them on the specifics of what is to be read for that particular service. Along with stressing the need for the

---

[79] Schmemann, *Great Lent*, p. 40.

readers to chant the readings in a clear manner, the choir director needs to caution the second reader to pause significantly after the chanting of the Second Prokeimenon, to allow the main celebrant to come out of the sanctuary with the candle and censer to proclaim, "The light of Christ illumines all!" Once the main celebrant re-enters the sanctuary and the deacon (or priest) intones, "Wisdom!", the second reader then proceeds with the second Old Testament reading, beginning with, "The Reading is from Proverbs!"

"Let My Prayer Arise"

After the second reading from the Old Testament, "Let My Prayer Arise" is celebrated. Even though the service books call for the priest or a reader to chant the verses from this (which is **still** done this way in the Antiochian tradition), in **most** parishes, it is customary for these verses to be **sung**, either by a single chanter, a trio, or all the singers.

What needs to be mentioned here is that this is a **repeating** of the verses for "Let My Prayer

Arise," the first time being immediately after "Lord, I Call Upon You" was sung. The reason for this repetition may be that, in the early Church, before the service was fully developed and consisted only of the distribution of Communion at Vespers, this second singing of the hymn was probably done as the Communion Hymn at the time of the partaking of the Eucharist. Now, it functions as a **penitential** introduction to the second part of the service, the Liturgy of the Presanctified Gifts proper.[80] Therefore, the singing of these verses, whether by a single chanter, a trio, or all the singers, should be done in a softly reverent, solemn, and penitential manner.

Litanies

After the short version of the Prayer of St Ephraim of Syria is done, there follow the litanies that precede the Eucharistic Entrance. These may consist of the Augment Litany, the Litany for the Catechumens, the Litany for Those Preparing for

---

[80] Ibid, p. 57.

Illumination (during the second half of Great Lent only), and/or the Litanies of the Faithful. In whatever combination they are done according to the local practice, whichever litanies are celebrated should, like all litanies, be done in a manner in which the petitions are not covered over but fully heard so they may be appropriately responded to by the people in the sung petitions.

"Now the Powers of Heaven"

Following the last Litany for the Faithful, the people sing the Entrance hymn, "Now the Powers of Heaven!". As with the singing of the Cherubic Hymn at a regular Divine Liturgy, this hymn is sung in two sections. The first consists of the text, "Now the Powers of Heaven do serve invisibly with us! Lo! The King of glory enters! Lo! The mystical Sacrifice is upborne, fulfilled!" Unlike a regular Divine Liturgy, there are **no** commemorations made during this Entrance. It is done in silence. Therefore, as will also be the case at the Entrance at the Vesperal Liturgy of Holy Saturday, there is **no** "Amen." sung before the second portion of the hymn continues. Instead, when the main celebrant quietly intones, "Let us draw near...!", the people sing, "Let us draw near in faith and love, and become communicants of life eternal! Alleluia! Alleluia! Alleluia!".

However, since there are **no** commemorations made during this Entrance, what was said concerning the Entrance Hymn at a regular Divine Liturgy can apply here as well: that is, after singing, "The mystical Sacrifice is upborne, fulfilled!", a reader may chant, one at a time, the verses from Psalm 23. The people can respond after each verse by singing the short refrain, "The mystical Sacrifice is upborne, fulfilled!" Again, the restoration of incorporating the **full** **Psalm** for the Entrance Hymn is to be encouraged.

The Litany Before the Lord's Prayer

Since this is the last litany preceding both the Lord's Prayer **and** the receiving of Holy Communion, it is imperative that this litany be celebrated in its entirety, with no abbreviations or omitted petitions whatsoever.

The Lord's Prayer

Being the Prayer of our Lord, Jesus Christ Himself, to God the Father, the singing of the Lord's Prayer must be done with the utmost reverence and solemnity.

"One is Holy!" and the Communion Hymn

"One is holy!" is then sung, followed by the *fixed* Communion Hymn, "O taste and see that the Lord is good! Alleluia! Alleluia! Alleluia!" This, also, should be sung reverently and solemnly.

Holy Communion

After the Prayer of Communion, "I believe, O Lord, and I confess,...!", the *clergy* partake of the Eucharist. As with the regular Divine Liturgy, it is encouraged here to, again, restore the celebration of the _**full**_ **Psalm**. As it was a moment ago after "One is holy!", the _**fixed**_ Communion Hymn, "O taste and see that the Lord is good!" from Psalm 33 is called for. After the people sing the entire verse, "O taste and see that the Lord is good!", the reader can chant, one at a time, the verses of Psalm 33. In between, the people sing the entire Psalm verse as a refrain.

After the clergy finish partaking of the Eucharist, the deacon intones, "In the fear of God, and with faith and love, draw near!", and the people respond by singing, "I will bless the Lord at all times! His praise will always be on my lips!"

Following this, the **people** then partake of the Eucharist. As was done for the clergy partaking, the _**full**_ **Psalm** practice of singing the Psalm verse refrain, interspersed with the chanting of the verses of Psalm 33, should be done. When _all_ have partaken of the Eucharist and the main celebrant chants, "Lo! This has touched your lips, has taken away all your iniquities, and cleansed you of all your sins!", the people then conclude by singing, "Alleluia! Alleluia! Alleluia!" Restoring this practice not only hearkens back to the practice of the early Church, but it also manifests the *unity* of the clergy and laity by celebrating the Communion Hymn in the same way for both!

Liturgy Ending

The thanksgiving elements of the Liturgy Ending, "Taste the heavenly Bread and the Cup of life!", "Let our mouths be filled!", and the Litany of Thanksgiving, are all elements of this liturgical "block" that concludes the part of the service that is the Eucharist proper. **Therefore**, in order to manifest this unity of liturgical elements, it would be most appropriate to sing this liturgical "block" in the *same melodic setting* as the Communion Hymn setting of Psalm 33 (the one exception being the Litany of Thanksgiving, which should be sung, where it is the local practice, in the Lenten melody)!

"Blessed be the Name!", Dismissal, and Recessional Hymns

The concluding liturgical elements are done in the Lenten melody, where practiced. Also, the local custom should be followed regarding the singing of recessional hymns as the people come forward to venerate the Holy Cross and the icons.

D. BRIDEGROOM MATINS

Since the Lenten services of the Akathist to the Theotokos and Little Compline are quite straightforward and present no liturgical issues to be addressed, they will not be discussed here.

The same situation applies to the services for Lazarus Saturday and Palm Sunday. The only comment that needs to be stressed is the centrality and importance of both Lazarus Saturday and Palm Sunday in the theological, spiritual, and liturgical preparation that is essential for the celebration of the services of Holy Week. For the quintessential discussion of both Lazarus Saturday and Palm Sunday, one should read Fr Alexander Schmemann's book, ***Great Lent: Journey to Pascha***.[81]

    The first thing that needs to be said regarding the celebration of Bridegroom Matins is that this service is essential and central to the liturgical experience of walking with our Lord to His Passion in the services of Holy Week. Some parishes, unfortunately, do not begin the Holy Week services until Thursday evening with the celebration of the Matins of Holy Friday with the Twelve Passion Gospels. These parishes that constrict their liturgical experience to that of "Holy Weekend" are missing vital liturgical elements that are part of the full, enriching spiritual experience of Holy Week. Fortunately, most parishes **have** restored this complete liturgical ordo. It is our prayer that all parishes will eventually do so.

---

[81] Ibid, pp. 79-85.

The First Doxology, "O Heavenly King!", and the Trisagion Prayers

Another essential point to be made regards the beginning of the service. After the doxology and the "Amen," the reader chants "Glory to You, our God, glory to You!", "O Heavenly King!", and the Trisagion Prayers concluding with the Lord's Prayer. However, in some traditions, the "Glory to You, our God, glory to You!" and "O Heavenly King!" are done by the priest. There are many other instances in the services of Holy Week where one or another tradition moves what would be a liturgical element done by a layperson to that of the priest. This practice reflects the unfortunate perspective of clericalism, which believes that only those who are ordained to clerical orders are "valid" to celebrate the services. This doctrine goes totally against the dogmas and Holy Tradition of the Orthodox Church! In fact, it is a canon of the Church that, when celebrating the Divine Liturgy, if, after the main celebrant intones the doxology, "Blest is the Kingdom...", there are no *lay* people to respond with the "Amen," the Liturgy is stopped and the clergy disrobe and go home. It is clear that the *lay* people, being "a chosen race, a royal priesthood, a holy nation, God's own people" (1 Peter 2:9), **together with** the clergy, offer the Liturgy and *all* liturgical services to the Lord. **Therefore**, at this point and all others in the services of Holy Week where liturgical elements usually done by the laity have been transferred to the clergy, that it is **imperative** that these liturgical elements be restored to the laity, as is proper.

The 6 Psalms

Another point that needs to be stressed is the celebration of the Six Psalms at the various Matins services during Holy Week. Some parishes will only do a few of these Psalms, say, the first three one day and the second three the next day. While it is recognized that it is a physical challenge to attend and participate in all of the services of Holy Week, it must again be stressed that the use of the Psalter should **not** be abbreviated or abridged. Other elements can be modified, such as eliminating the repetition of stikhera and the celebration of Little Litanies. The liturgical use of the Psalter is of the earliest experience of the Church, and constitutes a *very* central place in the celebration of the services.[82] **Therefore**, the liturgical elements of the Psalter should be experienced in their entirety.

"Alleluia!" and Troparion

Following the singing of "Alleluia!" with the chanting of interspersed Psalm verses, the people sing the troparion three times, with a 'split' "Glory" interspersed in between. During this singing, the clergy do a *full* censing of the church building. Therefore, while the singing of the troparion should not be done in a dragging or plodding manner, it also needs not to be rushed. A steady, even pace to the singing will provide the time necessary for the full censing of the church to be done.

---

[82] Ibid, pp. 38-40.

Kathisma Readings from the Psalter and Kathisma Hymns

Kathisma readings from the Psalter, along with Kathisma hymns, are then done. However, in some traditions, this liturgical unit is diminished to just the singing of the Kathisma hymns, with the Kathisma readings eliminated altogether. Again, it must be stressed that the ancient practice of Psalm readings from the Scriptures should be preserved as an essential element in the liturgical services.

The Matins Gospel

In **some** parishes that do **not** celebrate the Liturgy of the Presanctified Gifts during Holy Week, the main celebrant will **add on** the Gospel reading from the Liturgy of the Presanctified Gifts to the Matins Gospel. This added Gospel reading from Liturgy of the Presanctified Gifts is **not** called for at the Bridegroom Matins. While it is always good to hear the readings from Scripture, these added Gospel readings really belong to the Liturgy of the

Presanctified Gifts. Therefore, the addition of these readings *can* be omitted for the pastoral concern of the length of the services.

The Kanon

The Kanon is a central and essential liturgical element in Matins. In some traditions, however, it is the practice to repeat the heirmos of the Kanon as a katavasia at the end of each ode. This is another element that can be reduced for the sake of service length. In many parishes, only the heirmos of Ode 9 is repeated as a katavasia, and functions as the conclusion of the Kanon in its entirety. This seems to be a preferable liturgical practice that should be encouraged.

Also, for the sake of service length, the Little Litany that follows the Kanon can also be eliminated without affecting the service detrimentally.

The Exapostilarion

It is the custom, in **many** parishes, for the Exapostilaria of Holy Week to be sung by either a single chanter, or, more commonly, by a trio. It is usually sung three times, with a 'split' "Glory" interspersed in between. The preferred practice is for the trio to stand in the center of the nave for the singing of the Exapostilarion.

The Praises

In **some** traditions, the verses of the Praises, Psalms 148, 149, and 150, are abbreviated. Again, the **full** chanting of the Psalm verses should be restored, especially in this case where the elimination of those verses shortens the service by less than a minute..

The Lesser Doxology

The Lesser Doxology then follows. In *some* traditions, the exclamation by the celebrant, "Glory to You, Who have shown us the light!", is eliminated. This should appropriately be restored, since the point made by the exclamation, that Christ is the Light of the world, is central both to Matins and to the Holy Tradition of the Church.

Again, for the pastoral concern for the length of the service, the Little Litany that follows can be justifiably eliminated.

The Apostikha then follows, with its interspersed Psalm verses.

Prayer, the Trisagion Prayers, and the Lord's Prayer

Following the Apostikha, a reader chants the prayer, "It is good to give thanks to the Lord, to sing praises to Your Name, O Most–High, to declare Your steadfast love in the morning, and Your truth by night!". In *some* traditions, this is assigned to the priest. As mentioned previously, this should be restored to the laity, especially as it serves as a liturgical "bridge" between the Apostikha and the Trisagion Prayers and Lord's Prayer that followed, both of which are chanted by a layperson.

Conclusion of the Service

The Prayer of St Ephraim of Syria and the Dismissal then follow. After any pertinent announcements, recessional hymns that are part of the local custom may be sung as the people come forward to venerate the Holy Cross and the icons.

E. MATINS OF HOLY THURSDAY

For the Matins of Holy Thursday, everything that it has in common with the Bridegroom Matins that we have addressed here (the laity chanting the opening prayers; the singing of the full Six Psalms; the restoration of the Kathisma readings; the possible omitting of the Gospel from the Presanctified Liturgy; the reduction of the katavasia on the Kanon; the restoration of the full Psalm verses on the Praises; the restoration of the exclamation for the Lesser Doxology; and the laity chanting the prayer immediately preceding the Trisagion Prayers) applies to the Matins of Holy Thursday, as well.

What is essential to address here about this service concerns the Rite of the Washing of the Feet. In *some* traditions, not only is this Rite eliminated, but this entire service is replaced with the celebration of the Unction Service. This practice tends to interrupt the liturgical flow of Holy Week. The preferred practice is to celebrate the Unction Service on the afternoon of the Fifth Sunday of Lent, and then to celebrate the Matins of Holy Thursday with all baptized Orthodox Christians being anointed with the Holy Chrism *also* at the end of *that* service. Furthermore, it really is an *essential* liturgical element to restore the Rite of the Washing of the Feet to the conclusion of the Matins of Holy Thursday. This manifests, **through liturgical experience**, the kenosis, humility, and condescension of our Lord to our humanity, to experience clearly what St Irenaeus said, "God **became <u>man</u>** so that man could become God!". The Son of God, taking on our sinful human nature without sinning Himself, shows Himself to be the quintessential example of both divine humility and showing divine love through the service of others. This is clearly articulated in the Gospel reading for the Rite of the Washing of the Feet (John 13:1-17), when our Lord tells His disciples, "Do you know what I have done to you? You call me 'Teacher' and 'Lord'. And you are right, for so I am. If I, then, your Lord and Teacher, have washed your feet, **you, also, ought to wash one another's feet!** For, I have given you an *example*, that you, also, should do *as I have done to You!*" (John 13:12-15). This divine kenosis that is shown by the Lord is a prelude to the supreme divine kenosis that He will show in His Passion, Crucifixion, and Burial. **Therefore**, it is an **essential** and **vital** liturgical element of the services of Holy Week, and should be appropriately restored!

F. VESPERAL LITURGY OF HOLY THURSDAY

The Doxology, "O Heavenly King!", and the Trisagion Prayers

Again, as with the other services of Holy Week, the doxological response of "Glory to You, our God, glory to You!" and "O Heavenly King!" should be restored to the laity chanting these prayers.

"Lord, I Call Upon You!" and Stikhera

The service books call for each of the five stikhera here on "Lord, I Call Upon You!" to be sung twice. This is a place where the pastoral concern for the length of the services and the heavy load of the consistent services of Holy Week justify "trimming" the singing of each of these stikhera to one time each. In fact, in *most* parishes, that is the standard practice today, and should be encouraged everywhere.

Prokeimena and Old Testament Readings

In *some* traditions, the Prokeimena are reduced to *only* the first verse that is then sung by the people, eliminating the accompanying verse. Since Holy Week involves a long procession of lengthy services, it is *not* recommended to augment these Prokeimena to include all the verses from the designated Psalm. *However*, it *is* recommended that the second verse of each Prokeimenon be restored, per the usual practice.

Also, this liturgical unit consists of two Prokeimena and three Old Testament readings. It is the standard practice, recommended here, that three different readers participate in this liturgical unit: a first reader for the First Prokeimenon and the reading from Exodus, a second reader for the Second Prokeimenon and the reading from Job, and a third reader for the reading from Isaiah.

Many parishes omit the Little Litany that follows, along with the singing of the troparion and kontakion of the day. This, also, is a place where the omission of these elements can serve to make the length of the service more doable.

Prokeimenon, Epistle, and "Alleluia!" Verses

Then follows the Third Prokeimenon, Epistle reading, and "Alleluia!" verses. Depending on the number of people present and available readers, this liturgical can be done either with a fourth reader or the first reader of the previous liturgical unit.

The Gospel reading for the Liturgy then follows.

Litanies

Various litanies then follow the Gospel reading, which may include the Augmented Litany, the Litany of the Catechumens, the First Litany of the

Faithful, and the Second Litany of the Faithful. Again, for the pastoral concern of service length and stress, the first three of this group (the Augmented Litany, the Litany of the Catechumens, and the First Litany of the Faithful) may **all** be **omitted**. This leaves just the Second Litany of the Faithful to be celebrated. By modifying this liturgical unit in this manner, this final litany can then be **done *in its entirety, including*** the ***full*** final prayer (not just beginning at, "that, guarded always by Your might") before the exclamation. This is a **much** preferred practice, rather than piling on litanies and petitions and then abbreviating the final prayer.

"Of Your Mystical Supper"

The full singing of this special Entrance Hymn ("Of Your Mystical Supper, O Son of God, accept me today as a communicant! For, I will not speak of Your Mysteries to Your enemies, neither, like Judas, will I give you a kiss! But, like the thief, I will confess You: 'Remember me, O Lord, in Your Kingdom!'".) is sung in its entirety before the Entrance. It is again sung in its entirety, followed by a triple "Alleluia!", after the Entrance. Again, for the pastoral concern for the length of Holy Week services, it is **not** recommended to expand this into a full Cherubikon, as is preferred at a regular Divine Liturgy.

The Anaphora

What has been previously been said about the centrality of the Anaphora, and the fact that the Liturgy and the Holy Gifts are offered by **all** the people, **both** clergy **and** laity, applies here: The Kanon of the Anaphora **must** and **should** be done **aloud** in its **entirety**!

The Hymn to the Theotokos

Even though, in **some** traditions, the people sing "All of Creation" as the Hymn to the Theotokos at this point, it is really more proper to sing Ode 9 of the Matins Kanon celebrated the previous evening, sung in the special tone 6 melody and that begins:

"Come, O faithful! Let us enjoy the Master's hospitality,....!".

Holy Communion

What was used as the Entrance Hymn, "Of Your Mystical Supper," is the Communion Hymn that is called for to be sung during the partaking of Holy Communion on the part of **both** the clergy **and** the laity. As with the situation with the Liturgy of the Presanctified Gifts, this practice manifests the **unity** of the clergy and laity by celebrating the Communion Hymn in the same way for both! This practice should be the standard-bearer everywhere.

"Having Beheld the Resurrection of Christ"

The prayer," "Having Beheld the Resurrection of Christ," chanted by the deacon following Holy Communion, is actually a **hymn** that is sung as Post-Gospel Stikhera at Resurrectional Matins. It is therefore recommended that this hymn be restored to the people to sing at this point, in the standard tone 6 melody. This gives the clergy time to prepare the Holy Gifts to be transferred to the Table of Oblation, and restores the increased participation of the laity to its rightful liturgical place.

Liturgy Ending

In place of singing, "We Have Seen the True Light" and "Let Our Mouths be Filled" for the Liturgy Ending, this service replaces both of those liturgical elements with the singing, again, of "Of Your Mystical Supper." This is **totally** appropriate and recommended, because it ties together the **liturgical unity** of the receiving of the **Eucharist** (which means, "**thanksgiving**") with the **thanksgiving-centered** elements of the Liturgy Ending. Here, more than in any other form of the Liturgy as it has come down to us, is this ancient unity between these liturgical elements clearly manifested.

Conclusion of the Service

The remainder of the service, including the Litany of Thanksgiving, the Dismissal, and the possible singing of recessional hymns, poses no questions as to the celebration of these liturgical units.

G. MATINS OF HOLY FRIDAY

Doxology Prayers and 6 Psalms

As mentioned earlier, the opening prayers after the Doxology should be restored to the layperson who will be chanting the Trisagion Prayers that follow.

Also, the full Six Psalms should be chanted. As we will see, there will be more appropriate opportunities to trim down liturgical elements in this very long service.

"Alleluia!", Troparion, and Little Litany

Though the troparion for this service is different from that of the Bridegroom Matins ("When the glorious disciples…" instead of "Behold! The Bridegroom comes at midnight!"), the format at both services is the same: the singing of "Alleluia!" interspersed with Psalm verses, followed by a triple singing of the troparion (interspersed with a 'split' "Glory") while the clergy do a full censing of the church building. Again, the singing of the troparion needs to be a little slowly without dragging.

Following the troparion and the censing, the rubrics call for a Little Litany. Here is an excellent place where an insignificant liturgical element can be eliminated throughout the entire service. By "insignificant" we do not mean it has no value, but, rather, that it is a generic liturgical unit that is not particular to the service at hand. Little Litanies can be found in just about **any** service of the Church, and eliminating them here will **not** detract from the specifics that are unique to this service. Again, from the viewpoint of liturgical theology, it makes **much** more sense to eliminate the Little Litanies rather than to omit the liturgical elements from the Psalter!

Antiphons

Following the 1st Passion Gospel, the first set of Antiphons is sung. Although the content of these Antiphons deal specifically with the theme of this service, our Lord's Passion and Crucifixion, they are quite numerous and, frankly, repetitious in content. Therefore, it can be pastorally justified to trim down some of these Antiphon units. Most of them are grouped into a unit of three Antiphons. Some parishes, for example, will have the people sing only the first of the three Antiphons and eliminate the second two. So, for instance, in the first unit, Antiphon 1 can be sung while eliminating Antiphons 2 and 3. In the next unit, Antiphon 4 can be sung while eliminating Antiphons 5 and 6. The one exception to this, later in the service, is to ***not*** eliminate Antiphon 15, which states, "Today He Who hung the Earth upon the waters is hung upon the Tree!". This Antiphon is usually sung in a melismatic setting because, during the singing of Antiphon 15, the Holy Cross is processed from the sanctuary, brought out into the nave, and attached to the tomb in the center of the church. Therefore, since the singing of this Antiphon and its content are so directly connected to the procession of the Holy Cross, it is vital that this particular Antiphon *not* be eliminated.

Kathisma Hymns

Following the Antiphon units, before the singing of the next Passion Gospel, there is a Little Litany (which, as we have said previously, can justifiably be eliminated) and a Kathisma Hymn. These Kathisma Hymns are relatively short and are connected with the theme of our Lord's Passion, so they should remain included in the service.

The Beatitudes

After the 6th Passion Gospel, the Beatitudes are sung. As we mentioned earlier in chapter 5,[83] the first few verses of the Beatitudes are sung; then, the deacon begins chanting a series of verses, in between which the people continue singing the remaining verses of the Beatitudes. This practice of singing the Beatitudes in this manner is preserved from the earliest days of the Church, and should *not* be eliminated or adjusted in any manner.

The Prokeimenon

Before the 7th Passion Gospel, there is a Prokeimenon, "They divide My garments among them! And, for My raiment, they cast lots!", with the accompanying verse, "My God, My God, look upon Me! Why have You forsaken Me?". Again, with the pastoral concern for the length of Holy Week services, it is best to keep this current practice

---

[83] Cf. above, pp. 74-75.

of the Prokeimenon and *not* attempt to augment the practice by introducing verses from the entire Psalm.

Psalm 50

Psalm 50 follows the 7th Passion Gospel, and is an essential element of Matins. Therefore, it *should* be chanted by the reader, as prescribed.

The Kanon, the Kontakion, and the Oikos

The Kanon is sung after the 8th Passion Gospel. The customary practice of alternating two readers, one for the troparia to be chanted and one for the refrain, clearly manifests the format of the Psalm verse-refrain unit, and should be encouraged. Even though the service books call for each ode to be sung twice and the troparia to be repeated three or six times, in *most* parishes, this is *not* done. Instead, each ode is ***sung once***, and each troparion is ***chanted once*** by a reader, with another reader chanting the refrain, "Glory to You, our God, glory to

You!" until the final troparion is chanted, and then the final refrain is a full "Glory,… now and ever…!". This elimination of repetitive elements helps keep the celebration of the service to a doable level.

After the 6th ode, the Kontakion is sung, followed by the Oikos. The Kontakion begins, After the reader chants the phrase, "Do not pass me by in silence, O You Who kept me pure!", the people sing the cadence phrase, in the same tone 8 of the Kontakion, "For, You are my Son and my God!". Singing the cadence phrase of the Kontakion at the conclusion of the Oikos clearly manifests liturgically their connection.

Another way to keep the service at a manageable length is to eliminate the repetition of each heirmos as the Katavasia at the conclusion of each ode. The one exception to this is to sing the heirmos of Ode 9, "More honorable than the Cherubim,….!", as its Katavasia, so as to function as the conclusion of the entire liturgical unit of the Kanon proper.

The Exapostilarion

Following the Kanon, the Exapostilarion is celebrated, in a special melody in tone 8 or tone 3. In *many* parishes, this is sung by a single chanter, or, more commonly, by a trio. The practice of the trio standing in the middle of the nave to sing the Exapostilarion is standard, and should be encouraged.

The Praises

The Praises (Psalms 148, 149, and 150) are then chanted by a reader. After the phrase, "Praise Him with lute and harp!", the people sing, in tone 3, "Israel, My first-born son,…!". The service books call for this stikheron to be sung twice, but, in *most* parishes, it is sung *only once*. Again, elimination of repetitive elements is a justifiable way to keep the service at a comfortable length.

The Lesser Doxology

The Lesser Doxology follows the 10th Gospel. The Doxology, with its central theme of Christ as the Light of the world, is a **very** central part of Matins and should **not** be eliminated or abbreviated in any way.

The Litany of Matins

The Litany of Matins is then celebrated, responded to in a **non**-Lenten melody. Being a full Litany with specific petitions, rather than a Little Litany, it makes liturgical sense to *not* eliminate this Litany from the service.

The Apostikha

The Apostikha follows the 11th Gospel. It consists of four stikhera, followed by a "Glory" stikheron and a "Now and ever" stikheron. With the small amount of stikhera called for, it is best *not* to abbreviate the Apostikha at all.

Prayer, the Trisagion Prayers, and the Lord's Prayer

After the 12th Gospel, there is a prayer ("It is good to give thanks to the Lord..."), followed by the Trisagion Prayers and the Lord's Prayer. As usual, these should be done by a reader in the center of the nave.

The Troparion, Augmented Litany, Dismissal, and Recessional Hymns

The people then sing the Troparion, in tone 4: "By Your precious Blood, You have redeemed us from the curse of the Law!" In *some* traditions, this is sung three times, but it is best to sing it only once, as the service calls for.

Then the Augmented Litany is chanted. Again, being a full Litany with specific petitions, it is best to **not** eliminate this Litany from the service.

The Dismissal is done in the usual, prescribed manner. This may be followed, per local custom, to recessional hymns being sung as the people come forth to venerate the Tomb and the icons.

H. ROYAL HOURS OF HOLY FRIDAY

Only two comments need to be said regarding the Royal Hours of Holy Friday. The first concerns its time of celebration. Usually, the Vespers of Holy Friday is served at about 3:00 pm. Although *some* traditions practice serving the Royal Hours at any time before the Vespers, it makes more pastoral sense to schedule the Royal Hours in the morning, say, at 9:00 am.

The other comment concerns the fact that, throughout the various Hours in the service, some stikhera are called for to be repeated. Again, for the sake of service length, it is best to eliminate repetitions and to celebrate the service with each liturgical unit being done once.

I. VESPERS OF HOLY FRIDAY

Doxology, Prayers, and Psalm 103

Again, the opening prayers after the Doxology should be restored to the layperson who will be chanting the Trisagion Prayers that follow. In *some* traditions, "O Heavenly King!", the Trisagion Prayers, and the Lord's Prayer are all omitted. It is preferable *not* to omit these liturgical elements, since, for one thing, they are a standard in the services going back to the earliest days of the Church and, for another, omitting them does not shorten the service by any considerable length. After the chanting of "Come, let us worship God, our King!...", the reader continues with Psalm 103.

"Lord, I Call Upon You!" and Stikhera

Though the service books call for 6 stikhera to be sung, the first one, in tone 1, "All creation was changed by fear...!", is called for to be sung twice. In

many parishes, however, it is **usually** sung **only once**. Therefore, there end up being 5 stikhera. This is an acceptable reduction, since it is *not* eliminating this stikheron totally, only its repetition.

Prokeimena, Readings, and "Alleluia!" Verses

After the Entrance Hymn, "Gladsome Light!", there is the Scriptural unit of the service comprised of the following: 1st Prokeimenon, reading from Exodus, 2nd Prokeimenon, reading from Job, reading from Isaiah, 3rd Prokeimenon, an Epistle reading from 1 Corinthians, and "Alleluia!" verses. In parish practice, this are usually done by various readers, as follows: 1st reader: 1st Prokeimenon and reading from Exodus; 2nd reader: 2nd Prokeimenon and reading from Job; 3rd reader: reading from Isaiah; 4th (or, again, 1st) reader: 3rd Prokeimenon, Epistle reading from 1 Corinthians, and "Alleluia!" verses.

In *some* traditions, there is a tendency to reduce the Prokeimena to just the first verse. Again, while we don't recommend augmenting the Prokeimena to the celebration of the entire Psalm because of the pastoral concern for the length and weight of Holy Week services, the elimination of the second verse of any of the Prokeimena should *not* be done. As mentioned previously, the use of the Psalter is a central and ancient practice in the services of the Church, and the elimination of the second Prokeimenon verse at any point reduces the service by only a few seconds.

The Gospel

The Passion Gospel reading for this service is a composite reading, taken from Matthew 27:1-38; Luke 23:39-43; Matthew 27:39-54; John 19:31-37; and Matthew 27:55-61. In *some* traditions, there is the practice of, when the final verses of the composite Gospel reading are chanted (Matthew 27:55-61), one of the priests exits the sanctuary and, taking down the figure of Christ from the crucifix in the center of the church, wraps it in a white cloth, carries it into the sanctuary, and places it on the Altar. While this doesn't affect the singing of the musical responses in any way, it needs be mentioned that this practice should be discouraged, for two reasons: one, it interrupts the flow of the Gospel reading, and, two, it makes the reading of the Gospel into a performance event, like a "show-and-tell." It would be better to do this removal and procession of the crucifix to the end of the service, say, before the Dismissal, while the people sing the troparion of the day. This will avoid the cumbersome interruption of the Gospel reading itself.

The Apostikha

Concerning the Apostikha, there are three different practices regarding the processing of the Shroud of the Lord. In the Antiochian tradition, the Shroud (Epitaphion, Platchenitsa) is processed to the middle of the church and placed on the Tomb during the singing of the tone 5 stikheron after the "Glory,...now and ever...!". In the Greek practice, this begins at the start of the Apostikha. In the Slavic tradition, this takes place towards the end of the service, with the singing of the Troparion, "The Noble Joseph!". While there may be reasons for the development of these various practices, liturgically speaking it makes more sense to follow the Slavic tradition, since the content of the Troparion, "The Noble Joseph," articulates in the very text of the hymn what is precisely taking place during the processing of the Shroud.

"The Noble Joseph!"

Again, if the processing of the Shroud takes place during the singing of "The Noble Joseph," the **longer** version of the Troparion should be sung, to give sufficient time for the procession to take place. The text of this longer version is, "The noble Joseph, when he had taken down Your most pure Body from the Tree, wrapped it in fine linen and anointed it with spices and placed it in a new tomb! Glory to the Father, and to the Son, and to the Holy Spirit! When You descended to death, O Life Immortal, You slew hell with the splendor of Your Godhead! And when, from the depths, You raised the dead, all the powers of Heaven cried out: 'O Giver of Life, Christ our God, glory to You!' Now and ever and unto ages of ages! Amen. The angel came to the myrrh-bearing women at the tomb, and said: 'Myrrh is fitting for the dead! But, Christ has shown Himself a Stranger to corruption!'".

Dismissal and Recessional Hymn

The Dismissal is then done according to the standard practice.

While there are various practices of singing recessional hymns, the following seems to be the most liturgically appropriate one. In **many** parishes, as everyone comes forward to venerate the icons, the Shroud, the Gospel Book, and the Holy Cross, the people sing a hymn to a special melody in tone 5: "Come, let us bless Joseph of eternal memory." This is a lamentation that brings home to the people the depth of our Lord's Passion and Crucifixion for us and our salvation.

J. MATINS OF HOLY SATURDAY

Doxology, Prayers, and the 6 Psalms

Again, the opening prayers after the Doxology should be restored to the layperson who will be chanting the Trisagion Prayers that follow. Also, as mentioned with the previous Matins services of Holy Week, the chanting of the *full* Six Psalms should *not* be abbreviated or abridged at all.

"God is the Lord!" and "The Noble Joseph!"

Following the Great Litany, "God is the Lord!" is done, and then the **longer** version of "The Noble Joseph" is sung. This is the more preferred practice at this point in the service.

The Stases of the Praises

In *some* traditions, before the singing of the Stases of the Praises, , the Kathisma Hymns, Psalm 50, and the Kanon (which *follow* the Praises in the other traditions) are done at this point, *before* the Praises. Since the Stases of the Praises is a *major* liturgical element *unique* to this service alone, it seems to be liturgically more sensible to give it preference in the service, celebrating it at this point, and *then* to do the Kathisma Hymns, Psalm 50, and the Kanon (which are standard liturgical elements at regular Matins services throughout the rest of the year) *after* the Stases of the Praises.

Also, between the 1st and 2nd Stases, and again between the 2nd and 3rd Stases, a Little Litany is often done. Here, again, these Little Litanies *can* be eliminated without removing any liturgical elements central to the service.

Concerning the Stases themselves, it is customary in most traditions for the main celebrant (priest or bishop) to chant a series of troparia (as is done with the Kanon at Matins), and then the sung verses of Psalm 118 are interspersed with these troparia. Also, in *some* traditions, at the conclusion of each Stasis, the first troparion is repeated. This repetition can appropriately be eliminated. In *many* traditions, the interchange of the main celebrant chanting the troparia interspersed with the people singing the Psalm verses is *not* done for Stasis 3. Rather, the people sing the *entire* Stasis, **both** troparia **and** Psalm verses. Neither practice is liturgically more appropriate than the other. The only concern for a parish should be if the singers are proficient enough and have the musical fortitude to sing the entire Stasis. If so, it is appropriate to sing the entire Stasis. If not, then the main celebrant-singers interchange would be preferable.

Kathisma Hymns, Psalm 50, and the Kanon

As outlined above, it is liturgically preferable to do the Kathisma Hymns, Psalm 50, and the Kanon *after* the Stases of the Praises.

Like the celebration of the Kanon at the other Matins services of Holy Week, it is pastorally preferable to *not* sing the heirmos of each ode as the Katavasia at the conclusion of the ode, except for Ode 9, where the Katavasia functions as the conclusion of the Kanon proper. Also, any celebration of the Little Litany after Odes 3 and 6 can be appropriately eliminated. A Little Litany **can** be done after the Kanon and before the singing of "Holy is the Lord our God!".

"Holy is the Lord our God!"

In *some* traditions, the people themselves sing "Holy is the Lord our God!", with **no** chanting of each petition beforehand by a deacon. It seems to be more liturgically appropriate, however, for the deacon to first chant the petition, with the people responding to it afterwards, in a liturgical "dialogue."

The Praises

Even though the celebration of the three Stases of Psalm 118 from earlier in the service, often called "the Lamentations", is also referred to as "the Praises", what is *usually* called "the Praises" at this point of Matins is celebrated here, as well. These are done in the usual, standard format.

The Great Doxology and Procession

The Great Doxology is then sung, concluding with the Trisagion. After the "Glory,…now and ever…" and "Holy Immortal! Have mercy on us!", the slow, processional "Holy God!" is sung as the clergy and the people process around the church building once, with the Shroud in the center of the procession.

"The Noble Joseph"

After returning to the inside of the church building, the people sing the *shorter* version of "The Noble Joseph," as follows: "The noble Joseph, when he had taken down Your most pure Body from the

Tree, wrapped it in fine linen and anointed it with spices and placed it in a new tomb!"

The Troparion of the Prophecy

The people then sing the Troparion of the Prophecy, in tone 2: "O Christ, Who hold fast the ends of the Earth, You have consented to be held fast in the tomb, to deliver man from his fall into hell, and, as Immortal God, You have given us life and immortality!". The service books then call for a reader to chant a full "Glory,... now and ever...!", and then the people to repeat the singing of "O Christ, Who hold fast the ends of the Earth,...!". **However**, in **most** parishes, this Troparion of the Prophecy is sung **only once**, with*out* the intervening chanting of the "Glory,... now and ever...!". Given the weariness of all the people at this point of celebrating the marathon services of Holy Week, this singing of the Troparion **only once** seems to be pastorally preferable.

Prokeimenon 1 and the Reading from Ezekiel

There is then Prokeimenon 1 ("Arise, O Lord, and help us! Deliver us for Your Name's sake!"), followed by the "dry bones" reading from Ezekiel 37. In *some* parishes, the reader chanting this reading is proficient of ability to modulate his or her voice to higher notes for the parts of the reading where God is addressing Ezekiel, and to lower notes for the rest of the reading. While this is totally appropriate, caution needs to be exercised so that the elaboration of vocal changes does not become overdone to turn the reading itself into some sort of operatic performance on the part of the reader.

Prokeimenon 2 the Epistle Reading, and the "Alleluia!" Verses

After this, Prokeimenon 2 ("Arise, O Lord my God! Lift up Your hand! Forget not Your poor forever!") is chanted by a different reader, with responses sung by the people. This second reader then reads the Epistle composite reading that is from

1 Corinthians and Galatians. It is important that the reader understands that for this Epistle reading, being a composite reading (which is read as though it were one continuous text), the reader does **not** make a separate announcement of the reading at the point that the portion from Galatians begins. Rather, he or she **only** announces, at the beginning of the entire composite reading, "The Reading is from the First Epistle of the holy Apostle Paul to the Corinthians!".

The "Alleluia!" verses are then celebrated. Since there are **three** "Alleluia!" verses instead of the customary two, the celebration of these verses is as follows: The celebrant intones, "Peace be with you, Reader!", and then the reader chants, **all together**, "And with your spirit! Alleluia! Alleluia! Alleluia! Let God arise! Let His enemies be scattered! Let those who hate Him flee from before His Face!"

The Augmented Litany and the Litany of Supplication

Following the reading of the Matins Gospel (Matthew 27:62-66), the service calls for the Augmented Litany and the Litany of Supplication. Again, for pastoral concerns for the length and weight of the Holy Week services, it may be preferable to celebrate only the Augmented Litany (which contains specific petitions for the departed and living members of the parish community), and to eliminate the Litany of Supplication altogether. This will *not* adversely affect the celebration of this service whatsoever.

Dismissal and Recessional Hymn

The Dismissal is then done as prescribed. In *many* parishes, as the people come forward to venerate the Tomb, the Shroud, the Gospel Book, and the icons, a hymn to a special melody is sung: "Come, let us bless Joseph of eternal memory." This is a *very* appropriate hymn to sing at this point, since it functions in the same manner as singing "The Last Kiss" does at a funeral, when the people come forward for their final farewell to the newly departed person.

K. VESPERAL LITURGY OF HOLY SATURDAY

Although the service books call for the Vesperal Liturgy of Holy Saturday to be celebrated that day at about 4 o'clock in the afternoon, depending on the parish and the availability of parishioners to celebrate the service, it **may** begin as early as 10 o'clock in the morning. **Note:** Since the canons of the Church forbid the celebration of the Eucharist on Holy Saturday, the feast of Pascha itself, the Feast of feasts, is so full that it functions as <u>two</u> <u>days</u>: Pascha itself, <u>**and**</u> Bright Sunday. Therefore, Pascha has <u>**two Liturgies celebrated**</u> on it: the Vesperal Liturgy of Holy Saturday (and, Vespers is <u>**always**</u> considered the liturgical beginning of the **next** day!) <u>**and**</u> the Divine Liturgy that follows Paschal Matins. Therefore, the Vesperal Liturgy of Holy Saturday is really <u>**the first Paschal service**</u>! In many parishes, the Liturgy is celebrated in the center of the church, on the Tomb of Christ.

Doxology, Prayers, and Psalm 103

Again, the opening prayers after the Doxology should be restored to the layperson who will be chanting the Trisagion Prayers that follow. In *some* traditions, "O Heavenly King!", the Trisagion Prayers, and the Lord's Prayer are all omitted. It is preferable *not* to omit these liturgical elements, since, for one thing, they are a standard in the services going back to the earliest days of the Church and, for another, omitting them does not shorten the service by any considerable length. After the chanting of "Come, let us worship God, our King!...", the reader continues with Psalm 103.

"Lord, I Call Upon You!" and Stikhera

The fifth stikheron sung after "Lord, I Call Upon You!" and "Let My Prayer Arise" is called for to be sung **twice**: "Today, hell cries out, groaning: 'I should not have accepted the Man Born of Mary!'". Following the second singing of this stikheron, there are two more stikhera before the "Glory" stikheron. It is appropriate for the repeating of this fifth stikheron *not* to be eliminated, for two reasons. One, as can be seen, the content of this stikheron is **central** to our Lord's Passion and His victory over hell. Two, with the repetition of this stikheron, there are then eight stikhera before the "Glory" stikheron. The number **eight**, as we know, is the eschatological number of the Kingdom of God, the day of Sunday, of the Resurrection of Christ, the **first** day of the week, yet also the **eighth** day, the day beyond the seven days of this world, pointing to the **fulfillment** of all things in the Kingdom of God.[84] And since, as we said above, this is the first Paschal service of the Feast of feasts, it is appropriately symbolic to be singing **eight** stikhera at this point.

The 15 Old Testament Readings

Following the singing of "Gladsome Light," the 15 Old Testament readings are done. These readings

---

[84] Schmemann, *Great Lent*, p. 67.

are a ***central*** and ***essential*** feature of this service for the feast, showing, in encapsulated form, the fulfillment of all the Old Testament history and prophecies in Christ! Therefore, it is ***very*** important that these readings be done in the center of the nave of the church by competent readers in the parish.

Being the first Paschal service, it is hoped that the majority of the membership of the parish community will be present for the service. Therefore, it is highly recommended that ***fifteen different* lay people** do these readings! Naturally, these people need to prepare the readings ahead of time. As has been said, it is usually the choir director who is in charge of training and assigning readers in a parish. What seems to work well in *many* parishes is for the choir director to provide a sign-up sheet for these readings ***at the very beginning of Great Lent***. Keeping the sign-up sheet from the previous year available or, better yet, in the first column of the sign-up sheet and the availability for the readings for the current year in the second column, will ensure that different people have a chance to do the various readings from year to year. Also, running off the readings and stapling them in fifteen different packets, with the name of the church parish stamped on the back of each sheet of each packet, these readings can then be made available for the readers to go over and practice these readings throughout the Lenten season. If a reader is having difficulty with the pronunciation of a proper name or place, he or she can consult the choir director as to the correct pronunciation. Marking the parish name on the packets will make it more likely that the packets will be returned to the choir director, in order to make them available to new readers the following year. This is an **_excellent_** opportunity for the lay believers and faithful of the parish to **_actively_** and **_directly_** take part in a **_very central_** liturgical element of the service, and this should be highly encouraged, organized, and carried out each year!

One final point needs to be addressed. Both reading 6 and reading 15 involve, towards the end of the reading, the interaction of the reader with the people singing a refrain. Reading 6 concludes with the Song of Moses, where the people respond with the refrain, "For, gloriously has He been glorified!" Reading 15 concludes with the Song of the Three Youths in the fiery furnace, and the people sing the refrain, "Praise the Lord! Sing and exalt Him throughout all the ages!" Therefore, the two readers doing these two readings need to be **_very_** proficient and be able to interact with the singing of the people. Also, in many parishes, the singing of the refrains is done consistently in a manner that covers up the concluding sections of the two readings. This practice needs to be discouraged. What is a better method for doing this is, at the time the reader announces the refrain within his or her reading, the people sing the refrain once. Then, in a prearranged format, the reader can read anywhere from three to five verses, pause while the people again sing the refrain, and then proceed with another three to five verses before the refrain is sung again. This way, the content of the reading is not buried under the singing of the refrain, and the ancient practice of Psalm-verse-and-refrain is done in the appropriate manner.

The Prokeimenon, the Epistle, and "Arise, O God!" and Verses

After the Little Litany and the singing of "As Many As Have Been Baptized Into Christ," the main reader for the service goes to the center of the nave for the Scriptural block of liturgical elements. The Prokeimenon ("Let all the Earth worship You and praise You! Let it praise Your Name, O Most High!")

is done, followed by the Epistle reading from Romans.

Then, in place of the usual "Alleluia!" verses, there is the chanting of "Arise, O God! Judge the Earth!" with its accompanying verses. Between the Psalm verses chanted by the reader, the people sing the refrain of "Arise, O God!" As was the case with the 6th and 15th Old Testament readings, in many parishes the singing of "Arise, O God!" is done simultaneously with the Psalm verses, so that these Psalm verses are covered over and buried underneath the singing. An application of micro liturgics is called for here. During the celebration of "Arise, O God!", various people in the sanctuary and the nave go about and replace the purple lampadas and altar and analoi coverings with the white ones that will remain for the duration of the Pascha season. Time needs to be allowed for these changes to take place. **_Therefore_**, doing the Psalm verses and the refrain in an **_alternating_** manner, with the reader chanting a Psalm verse and **_then_** the people singing a refrain before the reader proceeds with the **_next_** Psalm verse, not only allows all the Psalm verses to be heard and understood, but **_also_** slightly lengthens the time needed for all the verses and refrains to be completed and, therefore, provides more time for the lampadas and coverings to be changed. *If*, after completing the last Psalm verse and refrain, the lampada and coverings changes have not finished, the reader can, ahead of time, be instructed to go back to the first Psalm verse, chant that with its accompanying refrain, and continue until all the lampada and coverings changes have been made. The reader can be previously instructed to keep one eye on the choir director, who, when it is time to finalize the last Psalm verse, can give a nod to the reader to complete the process at that time.

The Augmented Litany and the Litanies of the Faithful

Following the Gospel reading, the Augmented Litany and the Litanies of the Faithful are done. What was said concerning the elimination of the First Litany of the Faithful at the Vesperal Liturgy of Holy Thursday may also be applied here. This leaves just the Second Litany of the Faithful to be celebrated. By modifying this liturgical unit in this manner, this final litany can then be done *in its entirety, including* the *full* final prayer (not just beginning at, "that, guarded always by Your might") before the exclamation. This is a **much** preferred practice, rather than piling on litanies and petitions and then abbreviating the final prayer.

"Let All Mortal Flesh Keep Silent!"

Then the Entrance Hymn, "Let All Mortal Flesh Keep Silent!" is sung. As with the Entrance at the Liturgy of the Presanctified Gifts during Great Lent, ***this*** Entrance, on Holy Saturday, is done ***in complete silent***, with **no** commemorations made! ***Therefore***, as the title of the Entrance Hymn suggests, "Let All Mortal Flesh Keep ***Silent!***"), the first portion of the Hymn (***before*** the Entrance) should be sung through ***only once***, and then ***the singing stops!*** The second portion of the Hymn (***after*** the Entrance) does ***not*** begin with an "Amen.", since **no** commemorations have been made! ***Instead***, the people ***immediately*** take up the singing with, "Before Him go the ranks of angels,…!".

The Hymn to the Theotokos

Following the Anaphora is the Hymn to the Theotokos. In *some* traditions, the regular Hymn to the Theotokos from the Liturgy of St Basil the Great, "All of Creation!", is sung. It is actually more appropriate liturgically to do what is done in *most* other traditions, to sing Ode 9 of the Matins Kanon celebrated the previous evening, sung in the special tone 6 melody and that begins: "Do not lament Me, O Mother, seeing Me in the tomb, the Son, Conceived in the womb without seed! For, I will arise and be glorified with eternal glory as God! I will exalt all who magnify you in faith and in love!". As can be seen, the content of *this* particular Hymn to the Theotokos fits perfectly with the thematic content of this unique liturgical service.

Holy Communion

Since the Communion Hymn for the time of the laity to receive the Eucharist is the same as at a regular Sunday Divine Liturgy, what was said in chapter 5 regarding the restoration of the Koinonikon can very appropriately be applied here. Again, using the same Koinonikon for the receiving of Holy Communion by **both** the clergy **and** the laity will manifest the **unity** of all the Orthodox in the one Bread and the one Cup of the Eucharist!

"Having Beheld the Resurrection of Christ"

The prayer," "Having Beheld the Resurrection of Christ," chanted by the deacon following Holy Communion, is actually a **hymn** that is sung as Post-Gospel Stikhera at Resurrectional Matins. It is therefore recommended that this hymn be restored to the people to sing at this point, in the standard tone 6 melody. This gives the clergy time to prepare the Holy Gifts to be transferred to the Table of Oblation, and restores the increased participation of the laity to its rightful liturgical place. Furthermore, with what was said above about this being the first Paschal service, singing "Having Beheld the Resurrection of Christ" at this point will manifest that connection even more clearly.

L. NOCTURNS OF HOLY SATURDAY

Doxology, "O Heavenly King!", the Trisagion Prayers, the Lord's Prayer, "Come, Let Us Worship!", and Psalm 50

Again, the opening prayers after the Doxology should be restored to the layperson who will be chanting the Trisagion Prayers that follow. In *some* traditions, this entire section is omitted. It is preferable *not* to omit these liturgical elements, since, for one thing, they are a standard in the services going back to the earliest days of the Church and, for another, omitting them does not shorten the service by any considerable length.

The Kanon

The main liturgical element of this service is the Kanon. Just a few comments need to be addressed here.

First of all, even though a Little Litany is called for after the 3rd and 6th odes of the Kanon, it is best to eliminate them. By this point in Holy Week, everyone is *very* tired, and the fact that this service, which begins the Paschal Vigil and Divine Liturgy that follows begins around 11:30 pm on Saturday night, just adds to the exhaustion of all those present. Therefore, **any viable** elements that can be eliminated, such as this, should be.

Another directive calls for the Kathisma Hymn that follows the 3rd ode ("The soldiers guarding Your tomb, O Savior,…!") to be repeated after a full "Glory,…now and ever…!". Again, this repetition can justifiably be eliminated.

In *some* traditions, the Kontakion and Oikos that follow the 6th ode are eliminated. This is *not* recommended, since they are key liturgical elements within the Kanon.

Finally, *most* parishes repeat the heirmos of the 9th ode ("Do not lament Me, O Mother,…!") as the Katavasia. Since this functions as the conclusion of the Kanon proper, it is recommended that this practice remain in place.

The Trisagion Prayers and the Lord's Prayer

In *some* traditions, the priest chants the Trisagion Prayers and the Lord's Prayer. This is really a standard function for a layperson, and should *not* be taken from them to give to one of the clergy, who, honestly, have more than enough to do during this Vigil service.

The Troparion

The same situation occurs for this Troparion: in *some* traditions, it is given to the priest to chant. Being part of the hymnology of the Church, it is obvious that the proper procedure is to have the people sing it, as called for.

The Augmented Litany

In *some* traditions, this particular Augmented Litany is eliminated. In this case, that decision seems to make good sense. The Augmented Litany will be celebrated at both the Paschal Matins and the Paschal Divine Liturgy that follow, so eliminating it from the Nocturns would not deter from experiencing it later, but would only assist both in the pastoral concern for keeping the services at a comfortably managable length and for moving the liturgical pace of Nocturns smoothly forward. The Dismissal then follows, and all lights within the church building are extinguished before the beginning of Paschal Matins.

M. PASCHAL MATINS

"Come, and Receive the Light!"

Following the Dismissal of Nocturns and the extinguishing of the lights and candles, there are a few moments of silence. Then, the main celebrant lights one candle and, coming out of the sanctuary and standing on the ambo of the solea, he chants, sometimes in a special melody, "Come, and receive the Light that is never overtaken by the night!

Come, and glorify the Christ, Who is Arisen from the dead!" This is a practice that is being restored in many parishes and, with the centrality in our liturgical services of emphasizing Christ as the Light of the world, it is a practice that should definitely be encouraged.

"Your Resurrection!"

Then, the singing of "Your Resurrection!" commences, in tone 6. This is done in different ways in various parishes. It **may** start out as a quartet of men in the sanctuary, singing it **three** times (softly, medium volume, and then, the third time, loudly), before the rest of the congregation sings it. It **may** start out with just a choir singing it, and then the rest of the people in the parish joining in. In any case, this hymn is sung continuously throughout the triple procession around the church building. This is a standard practice in all the liturgical traditions.

The Doxology and "Christ is Risen!" with the Paschal Verses

After the Doxology, "Glory to the Holy, consubstantial, life-creating and undivided Trinity, always now and ever and unto ages of ages!", the Troparion of Pascha, "Christ is Risen!", is sung with the alternating verses from Psalm 67:1-3 and Psalm 117:24. Again, this is a standard practice in all the traditions.

The Matins Gospel

Even though the service books call for it to be celebrated **before** the Doxology, the Paschal Troparion, and the Paschal Verses, **many** parishes will celebrated the chanting of the Matins Gospel at this point, **after** those initial liturgical elements (which, actually, makes more sense liturgically). The Matins Gospel called for here is the 2nd of the 11 Resurrectional Matins Gospels, Mark 16:1-8 (in the Greek practice, the Gospel reading is Matthew 28:1-20) . The chanting of this Matins Gospel is part of the **Byzantine** tradition and **not** often a part of the **Slavic** tradition. **However**, more and more parishes of the **Slavic** tradition are embracing the chanting of this Gospel, which is a good thing, since, by omitting it, it seems to be the **<u>only</u>** Matins service *of the entire liturgical year* that is celebrated with**out** a Matins Gospel!

The Great Litany

The service books then call for the Great Litany to then be celebrated, with its usual responses. However, **many** parishes, noting that the Great Litany is also called for at the beginning of the Paschal Divine Liturgy, will **omit and eliminate** it either here or at the beginning of the Paschal Divine Liturgy. This seems to be a wise choice, since the repetition of this litany at either point will only serve to prolong what is already a very long service. It may be preferred to eliminate this litany at the beginning of the Paschal Divine Liturgy. The reason for that is, by doing it here at the beginning of Paschal Matins, it gives everyone still coming in from the outdoor procession to come in and get settled in their place in the church building.

The Kanon

The Kanon then follows. Being Pascha, the Feast of feasts, **_every_** part of the Kanon is sung! Therefore, there is **_no_** chanting of troparia by a reader. Rather, the troparia are sung in the same melody as the odes of the Kanon. In **_some_** traditions, only the heirmoi of the odes are sung, and the troparia are eliminated. This is **_not_** a preferable practice! Again, Pascha being the Feast of feasts and the center of the liturgical year, **_everything_** that is **_essential_** to the service, including these troparia, should be celebrated! In contrast to that, minor liturgical elements that are **_not_** festal elements of the service, such as the Little Litanies called for after the 3rd and 6th odes, **_can_** be eliminated without sacrificing essential features of the feast.

Other essential festal elements, such as the Hypakoe after the 3rd ode and the Kontakion and

Oikos after the 6th ode, should be done. Even though the Synaxarion that is called for after the Oikos deals specifically with the theme of Christ's Resurrection, it **does** seem to interrupt the festive flow of the singing of the Kanon and can, therefore, be omitted.

The Post-Gospel Stikhera that follow, beginning with "Having beheld the Resurrection of Christ, let us worship the holy Lord, Jesus, the only sinless One!", are an essential part of the Paschal Matins (and, for that matter, the Resurrectional Matins celebrated throughout the rest of the liturgical year), and **must** be celebrated!

Regarding Ode 9, **many** parishes *only* sing the following **shortened** version of this Ode 9: "The angel cried to the Lady full of grace: 'Rejoice! Rejoice, O pure Virgin! Again, I say, "Rejoice!" Your Son is Risen from His three days in the tomb! With Himself, He has raised all the dead! Rejoice! Rejoice, O you people!' Shine! Shine! Shine, O new Jerusalem! The glory of the Lord has shone on you! Exult, now, exult, and be glad, O Zion! Be radiant, O pure Theotokos, in the Resurrection of your Son!". The following is the *longer* version that is called for:

Heirmos 1: "Shine! Shine! Shine, O new Jerusalem! The glory of the Lord has shone on you! Exult, now, exult, and be glad, O Zion! Be radiant, O pure Theotokos, in the Resurrection of your Son!"; Troparion 1: "How divine! How beloved! How sweet is Your voice, O Christ! For, You have promised faithfully to be with us to the end of the world! Having You as our Anchor of hope, we, the faithful, rejoice!"; Troparion 2: "O Christ, great and most holy Pascha! The Wisdom, Word, and Power of God, grant that we more perfectly may partake of You in the never-ending Day of Your Kingdom!"; Refrain 1: "My soul magnifies Him Who voluntarily endured death, was buried, and rose from the dead on the third day!"; Refrain 2: "My soul magnifies Him Who rose from the dead on the third day: Christ, the Giver of life!"; Refrain 3: "Christ, the New Pascha! The Living Sacrifice! The Lamb of God, Who takes away the sins of the world!"; Refrain 4: "Today, all creation rejoices and is glad! For, Christ is Risen, and He has despoiled hell!"; "Glory...Spirit!"; Refrain 5: "My soul magnifies the might of the indivisible and Tri-Personal Godhead!"; "Now and ever...Amen."; Refrain 6: "Rejoice, O Virgin, rejoice! Rejoice, O blessed one! Rejoice, O glorified one!

For, Your Son is Risen from His three days in the tomb!"; and, Refrain 7: "The angel cried to the Lady full of grace: 'Rejoice! Rejoice, O pure Virgin! Again, I say, "Rejoice!" Your Son is Risen from His three days in the tomb! With Himself, He has raised all the dead! Rejoice! Rejoice, O you people!'". While it is more festive and liturgically fulfilling to sing the longer version, pastoral concerns for the length of the service are justified at this point. Therefore, whatever practice is pastorally more beneficial for the local parish community should be followed. For those parishes that sing the shorter version at this point, consideration may be made in singing the longer version of ode 9 during Clergy Communion at the Divine Liturgies of all the Sundays during the Paschal season. This way, **both** the longer **and** shorter versions are liturgically experienced, while still maintaining pastoral concern for service length. Finally, unlike Kanons celebrated on other feasts, the repeating of ode 9 as a Katavasia for the Kanon of Pascha should **not** be done.

In *some* traditions, a Little Litany is done following the Kanon, but this can be justifiably eliminated.

The Exapostilarion

As with the Exapostilarion at the Matins of Holy Friday, the Exapostilarion for Pascha is often done by a trio, a quartet, a quintet, or some other such small group of singers. It *is* liturgically proper and appropriate to sing this in the center of the nave of the church.

The Praises and "Let God Arise!"

Following the Exapostilarion, the Praises are sung in tone 1: "Let every breath praise the Lord! Praise the Lord in Heaven! Praise Him in the highest! To You, O God, is due a song!", and, "Praise Him, all you angels of His! Praise Him, all His hosts! To You, O God, is due a song!". In the *some* traditions, this is followed by the first four Resurrectional stikhera of the Praises from tone 1. However, the singing of these seem to come off liturgically at this point as repetitious, and can and should be eliminated.

This is followed with the singing of the full verses of "Let God Arise!" Being such a **Paschal** element (remember! These verses compose what the main celebrant chants in between the singing of "Christ is Risen!" at the beginning of every service of the Paschal season!), these verses should be sung in the most joyous, assertive, and celebratory manner possible!

The Paschal Sermon and Troparion of St John Chrysostom

The Paschal Sermon of St John Chrysostom is then chanted by the priest. The Troparion of St John Chrysostom is then sung. Though this is not called for in the service books, it is **almost <u>always</u>** done in most parishes. This concludes Paschal Matins. The Paschal Divine Liturgy then begins **_immediately_** following.

N. PASCHAL DIVINE LITURGY

The Great Litany

Following the Doxology and the Paschal Troparion and Verses, the Great Litany is called for. As discussed in the previous section, since this litany was already celebrated at Paschal Matins and preserved there for the reasons already enumerated, it is preferable to eliminate the duplication of this litany at the beginning of the Paschal Divine Liturgy.

The Antiphons

The Antiphons, with "Only-Begotten Son" sung after the 2nd Antiphon, are then done in the prescribed manner. Being not only a great feast but the Feast of feasts, the Beatitudes are replaced in the 3rd Antiphon with the singing of the Paschal Troparion, "Christ is Risen!", alternated with Psalm verses chanted by a reader. The choir director needs to be sure to assign a seasoned and highly competent reader to this particular Divine Liturgy of all the Liturgies celebrated in the liturgical year.

The Hypakoe and the Kontakion

Following the Introit chanted by the deacon during the Entrance and the final singing of the Paschal Troparion, the Hypakoe is sung, followed by a full "Glory,…now and ever…" and then the Kontakion of Pascha. This is a standard format and practice in all the liturgical traditions.

"As Many As Have Been Baptized!"

Instead of singing the regular Trisagion ("Holy God!"), at this point, the people sing, "As Many As Have Been Baptized!". Again, this a standard format and practice in all the liturgical traditions.

The Gospel

Following the Prokeimenon, the Epistle reading, and the "Alleluia!" Verses, the Gospel reading from the Prologue of John is chanted. After the deacon or the priest read the Gospel, it is customary in **many** traditions to have lay people come forward who are proficient in various foreign languages to read this Gospel (or a portion of it) in their particular foreign language. This manifests the cosmic universality of the Gospel message of Christ's Resurrection. In **some** traditions, this multi-language reading of the Gospel is done the following morning or afternoon at Paschal Vespers. Though this can be a viable alternative, it is really more appropriate to do that here, at the time when this particular Gospel reading is **<u>already being done</u>** in Americanized English. This keeps the unity of the Gospel message clearly manifested.

The Augmented Litany and the Litanies for the Faithful

After the Augmented Litany, the two Litanies of the Faithful are called for. Again, as mentioned for previous Divine Liturgies of Holy Week, it may be preferable for pastoral reasons to omit the First Litany of the Faithful and take only the Second Litany of the Faithful with its full prayer of the exclamation.

The Cherubikon

What was presented in the earlier chapter on the Divine Liturgy regarding the Cherubikon *can* be applied here. Celebrating it in the ancient Psalm-verse-and-refrain format, with the alternating verses of Psalm 24, will really not lengthen the service to any perceptible degree, and will once again give the clergy time to do their prayers, prepare the Holy Gifts, and then process out of the sanctuary for the Eucharistic Entrance. The choir director and the reader chanting the Psalm verses can both keep an eye on the sanctuary and cease any further Psalm verses once the procession of the Entrance begins, since liturgical commemorations *are* done at this Divine Liturgy.

The Anaphora

Following the Litany of Supplication, "Father, Son, and Holy Spirit," and the Creed, the Anaphora of St John Chrysostom is then celebrated. Again, the Anaphora is **the central** section of the Divine Liturgy! As such, being not only the central part of the service, but ***a corporate act, the Eucharistic prayers must be said aloud for all to hear and offer, in (again) this corporate worship!*** For the liturgical musician, then, it is imperative that all arrangements and musical settings of the Anaphora that incorporate long, melismatic singing that "covers over" the Eucharistic Kanon be avoided and eliminated. Being the essential and central part of the Divine Liturgy, with its victorious affirmation of the Holy Trinity and its emphasis on joy, praise, and thanksgiving, *all* settings of the Anaphora should be festive, celebratory, upbeat, joyous, and **paschal!**

The Hymn to the Theotokos

As with the singing of the 9th ode of the Kanon at Paschal Matins, here the **shortened** version of "The Angel Cried!" is usually sung as the Hymn to the Theotokos. Again, the **longer** version may be sung during Clergy Communion later in the service.

"One is Holy!" and the Communion Hymn

Following the Lord's Prayer, the people then sing, "One is holy!", followed **immediately** by the Communion Hymn. Here, for Pascha, the situation with the Communion Hymn is unique. For many feasts of the year that fall on a Sunday, the people first sing, "Praise the Lord from the Heavens! Praise Him in the highest!", and then sing the special Communion Hymn for the feast. For Pascha, however, the situation is reversed: The people **_first_** sing, "Receive the Body of Christ! Taste the Fountain of immortality!", **_then_**, they sing, "Praise the Lord from the Heavens! Praise Him in the highest!", and, **_then_**, sing a **triple** "Alleluia!". This will be the pattern for singing the Communion Hymn every Sunday through the Leavetaking of Pascha. In *some* traditions, "Praise the Lord from the Heavens!" is omitted, but this is *not* a preferred practice. Keeping all festive elements to a maximum for the Feast of feasts is more appropriate.

Holy Communion

A variety of practices may be employed for the time of Holy Communion. The aforementioned longer version of ode 9 from the Paschal Kanon may be sung during Clergy Communion. The ancient practice of the Koinonikon, with Psalm verses and refrain, may also be employed. Whatever is done, consistency and unity of the clergy and laity when approaching the chalice should be manifested in the liturgical practice used in the particular parish.

"Having Beheld the Resurrection of Christ

If ever a Divine Liturgy during the liturgical year would be most appropriate for the people to sing the **hymn**, "Having beheld the Resurrection of Christ", it is this Paschal Divine Liturgy! Along with properly being a hymn that **should** be sung in the prescribed tone 6, the singing of these verses also gives the clergy sufficient to prepare the Holy Gifts in the chalice and on the diskos to be transferred back to the Table of Oblation.

The Liturgy Ending and the Ending Litany

For the Liturgy Ending, when the celebrant intones, "O God, save Your people and bless Your inheritance!", the people do **_not_** sing, "We have seen the true Light!", but, **_instead_**, sing the full Troparion of Pascha, **once**: "Christ is Risen from the dead, trampling down death by death, and, upon those in the tombs, bestowing life!".

Then, when the celebrant intones, "Blessed is our God, always now and ever and unto ages of ages!", the people do **_not_** sing, "Let our mouths be filled...!", but, **_instead_, _again_** sing the full Troparion of Pascha, *once*: "Christ is Risen from the dead, trampling down death by death, and, upon those in the tombs, bestowing life!". **Some** traditions **do** sing "Let our mouths be filled...!" instead, but this seems **most** inappropriate for the Feast of feasts! The singing again of "Christ is Risen!" *is* preferred!

After this, there is the Ending Litany, and then "Blessed be the Name of the Lord!". In **some** traditions, this is replaced with the triple singing of "Christ is Risen!", which **is** a more appropriate practice, as it maximizes the festal elements of the Feast of feasts.

The Dismissal, and the recessional hymns are celebrated, with their appropriate responses.

O. PASCHAL VESPERS

The Doxology, "Christ is Risen!",
The Paschal Verses and Troparion

The celebrant intones the **_Matinal_** doxology, "Glory to the Holy, consubstantial, life-creating and undivided Trinity, always now and ever and unto ages of ages!". The people respond by singing, "Amen.". Then, the celebrant begins the Paschal verses, with "Let God arise! Let His enemies be scattered!...", and the people respond, after each verse, with the Paschal Troparion, "Christ is Risen!".

Unlike other forms of Vespers, Paschal Vespers does **_not_** then proceed with "Come, let us worship!" and Psalm 103. Rather, the service then goes directly to the Great Litany.

"Lord, I Call Upon You!" and Stikhera

Unlike Resurrectional Vespers celebrated on Saturday evenings throughout the year, there is no Kathisma 1 ("Blessed is the man…!") or any other Kathisma celebrated at Paschal Vespers. Instead, the people go from the conclusion of the Great Litany into immediately singing, "Lord, I Call Upon You!", in tone 2. There are then 6 stikhera sung. Again, since this is Paschal Vespers, **everything** is sung! In other words, there is **no** chanting of the interspersed verses by a reader. Therefore, after singing, "Let my prayer arise…!", the people sing, "If You, O Lord, should mark iniquities,…!", and then the stikheron in tone 2 that begins, "Come, let us worship the Word of God, begotten of the Father before all ages…!", etc.

"Gladsome Light" and the Great Prokeimenon

"Gladsome Light" is sung, as usual, as the Entrance Hymn. Then follows the Great Prokeimenon, "Who is so great a God as our God?

You are the God Who do wonders!". The people then sing this full Prokeimenon, "Who is so great a God as our God? You are the God Who do wonders!" to a special melody in tone 7. They sing this full Great Prokeimenon after the subsequent verses chanted by the deacon. In *some* traditions, the last verse by the deacon is abbreviated. Instead of chanting the full verse, "I remembered the works of the Lord! For, from the beginning, I will remember all Your wonders!", only the first sentence of this verse is taken. This seems to be an *in*appropriate practice. Again, for Pascha, the Feast of feasts, *everything* of a festal nature should be celebrated, and eliminating this last sentence does not shorten the service by any noticeable time length.

The Gospel

The Gospel reading for the Paschal Vespers, John 20:19-25, is then celebrated, with the usual responses. In *some* traditions, this Gospel reading is done in *three* sections, as follows: John 20:19-20; John 20:21-23; and John 20:24-25). This tends to fragment the Gospel reading, and is hardly recommended. Again, in *some* traditions, **this** is the time that the Gospel Reading from the Prologue of John then chanted in **various languages**. As mentioned previously, it is appropriate to do this the previous night, when this Gospel is called for.

The Apostikha, the Paschal Stikhera, and the Dismissal

The Apostikha follows the various litanies and "Vouchsafe, O Lord". The first Resurrectional stikheron from tone 2, "Your Resurrection, O Christ our Savior, has enlightened the whole universe, recalling Your creation! Glory to You, O Almighty Lord!", is sung, followed by the Paschal verses beginning, "Let God arise!".

Unlike other forms of Vespers, there is **no** inclusion here of St Symeon's Prayer, the Trisagion Prayers, the Lord's Prayer, and the troparion for the day. Rather, the service moves directly to the Dismissal and any recessional hymns that may be sung.

P. PASCHAL HOURS

The only comment to be made regarding the Paschal Hours is that **_everything_** is sung: **_nothing_** is to be chanted by a reader.

Q. BRIGHT WEEK

Only two liturgical comments need to be made regarding the various traditions of the all the services of Bright Week concerns the end of the Divine Liturgy. In **_some_** traditions, "Blessed be the Name of the Lord!" is sung three times at its appropriate place in the service. In **_other_** traditions, this is replaced with a triple singing of the Paschal Troparion, "Christ is Risen!". As previously stated, for Pascha and Bright Week only, the addition of the festal element of "Christ is Risen!" seems more appropriate.

The other comment regards the blessing of graves at the cemetery of the parish after the Divine Liturgy on Thomas Sunday. At the conclusion of the Memorial, when the celebrant intones "Memory Eternal!" for all the departed members of the parish community, it is **_more appropriate_** to replace the singing of "Memory Eternal!" on the part of the people singing with the festive "Christ is Risen!". Again, with Pascha being the Feast of feasts that is also the nexus of the liturgical year, **_all_** festal elements need to be maximized throughout Bright Week and the Pascha season!

9
DEVELOPMENT OF LITURGICAL THEOLOGY

With all of the different liturgical traditions of our Church with their variant elements, there is an urgent need in our time for a serious, well-informed, and theological development of our liturgical theology. Currently, there are three ways in which that can be done.

A. LITURGICAL RESEARCH

The first way is for Church liturgists to continue doing liturgical research. This can take two forms. One is to research, through various sources, what have been the more ancient, full, and authentic liturgical practices of the Church before other influences were brought to bear on our services (gradual development of expanded hymnology that replaced Psalmody, Western perspectives and practices, etc.). The other is to seek out, read, and assimilate the research that other scholars have done and have shared in their own particular writings. One person who comes to mind is the Byzantine scholar, Robert F. Taft, SJ. His deep and thorough research has been synthesized in his various writings that have been both published and embraced worldwide.

B. LITURGICAL PUBLICATIONS

The second way is for Orthodox liturgists, once they have done their own research, to synthesize their findings in the very same way as the aforementioned Robert F. Taft, by sharing the fruits of their research via books, articles, and other liturgical publications. Also, thanks to the technological development of our modern age, these scholars can share their knowledge through other venues and mediums, such as podcasts on Internet sites such as Ancient Faith Radio. This "passing on" of liturgical scholarship will then assist the cycle of liturgical development by providing the next generation of Orthodox liturgical researchers valuable information and insight towards deeper liturgical knowledge.

C. LITURGICAL SYMPOSIUMS

The third and final way is to provide venues for liturgical discussions via liturgical symposiums. In the early 1970's, St Vladimir's Seminary in New York established an annual summer event held the last week of June, called, "Institute of Liturgical Practices." It was a forum that provided the opportunity for Orthodox clergy and well-educated Church musicians to come together in a conference setting to share knowledge, ideas, and sources of liturgical information and research. Within a few years, the summer Institute evolved into a format whereby a theme of wide-range interest to the Orthodox at large was chosen for each annual gathering. Such themes included marriage, priesthood, and mission. This new format then coalesced into a form in which, after the initial Monday morning keynote address, those who had signed up for the "pastoral tract" remained in one meeting hall to discuss the specific theme chosen for that year, while those who signed up for the "musical tract" were relegated to another separate meeting place on the campus where they dealt with the topics and skills unique to their ministry, such as choir directing, study of the eight tones, etc.

While this served the function for necessary discussion on pertinent issues concerning the Church, the original format of liturgical discussions and development fell by the wayside. It seems that establishing a new venue that provides the opportunity for Orthodox clergy and trained Church musicians to once again come together to share knowledge, ideas, and sources of liturgical information and research, is a viable and necessary task that needs to be encouraged and reestablished. It is through this sound, educated, theological, and well-informed development of ideas, information, and research in the area of Orthodox liturgical theology that the authentic worship of the one, truly, and living God will be manifested in our Church, to the glory of God and His eternal Kingdom!

BIBLIOGRAPHY

Liturgical Books

Mother Mary and Ware, Archimandrite Kallistos, ***The Festal Menaion***, Faber and Faber, London, 1977.

_____, ***The Lenten Triodion***, Faber and Faber, London and Boston, 1978.

Books

Hopko, Thomas, ***The Orthodox Faith: Volume I: Doctrine,*** 2nd Edition, Department of Religious Education, Orthodox Church in America, SVS (St Vladimir's Seminary) Press, Yonkers, NY.

_____, ***The Orthodox Faith: Volume II: Worship,*** 2nd Edition, Department of Religious Education, Orthodox Church in America, SVS (St Vladimir's Seminary) Press, Yonkers, NY.

Lossky, Vladimir, ***The Mystical Theology of the Eastern Church***, SVS (St Vladimir's Seminary) Press, Crestwood, NY, 2002.

Meyendorff, John, ***Byzantine Theology: Historical Trends and Doctrinal Themes***, Fordham University Press, New York, NY, 1983.

_____, ***Marriage: An Orthodox Perspective***, SVS Press, Crestwood, NY, 1984.

Schmemann, Alexander, ***For the Life of the World: Sacraments and Orthodoxy***, SVS Press, Crestwood, NY, 2002.

_____, ***Of Water and the Spirit: A Liturgical Study of Baptism***, SVS Press, Crestwood, NY, 1974.

_____, ***Great Lent: Journey to Pascha***, SVS Press, Crestwood, NY, 1974.

_____, *Liturgy and Life: Christian Development through Liturgical Experience*, Department of Religious Education, Orthodox Church in America, New York, NY, 1983.

_____, *Liturgy and Tradition: Theological Reflections of Alexander Schmemann*, Thomas Fisch, Editor, SVS Press, Crestwood, NY, 1990.

_____, *The Eucharist: Sacrament of the Kingdom*, SVS (St Vladimir's Seminary) Press, Crestwood, NY, 1988.

Taft, Robert F., SJ, *The Great Entrance: The History of the Transfer of Gifts and other Preanaphoral Rites of the Liturgy of St John Chrysostom*, OCA 200, Rome, Italy, PIO, 1975.

_____, *Beyond East and West: Problems in Liturgical Understanding*, Second Revised and Enlarged Edition, Pontifical Oriental Institute, Rome, Italy, 2011.

Uspensky, Nicholas D., ***Evening Worship in the Orthodox Church***, translated and edited by Paul Lazor, SVS Press, Crestwood, NY, 1985.

Articles

Meyendorff, Dr. Paul, "Saturday Evening Worship: A Proposal", *Jacob's Well*, Newsletter of the Diocese of New York and New Jersey, Orthodox Church in America, Spring 1995 issue, p. 5.

www.ingramcontent.com/pod-product-compliance
Lightning Source LLC
Chambersburg PA
CBHW050105170426
43198CB00014B/2473